AMOS:
THE SHEPHERD PROPHET

AMOS: THE SHEPHERD PROPHET

Allan M. Harman

THE BANNER OF TRUTH TRUST

THE BANNER OF TRUTH TRUST

Head Office
3 Murrayfield Road
Edinburgh, EH12 6EL
UK

North America Office
PO Box 621
Carlisle, PA 17013
USA

banneroftruth.org

*

ISBN
Print: 978 1 84871 987 3
Epub: 978 1 84871 988 0
Kindle: 978 1 84871 989 7

*

Typeset in 11/15 Adobe Garamond Pro at
The Banner of Truth Trust, Edinburgh

Printed in the USA by
Versa Press Inc.,
East Peoria, IL.

To my friends and colleagues
of the Bellarine Prayer Fellowship:
John Cromarty, Peter Orchard, Rod Waterhouse,
and Robert White

Contents

Preface

The first book I read in its entirety in the Hebrew Bible was the book of Amos. It was in my second year as a theological student, and I still remember the delight when I could read through it in its original language in less than an hour. Now I have come back again to Amos, and this commentary is the result of my long acquaintance with it. Those who have used my other commentaries (on Exodus, Deuteronomy, Psalms, and Isaiah, Christian Focus Publications, or that on Daniel, Evangelical Press) will not be surprised by the format of this book.

Anyone who writes on a biblical book like Amos has to acknowledge indebtedness to all those who have previously ventured on its exegesis, as I gladly do. The absence of numerous references to others is not to slight them, but rather stems from my conscious decision not to clutter up the text with debates with them. I wanted to set out my understanding of the text without the distraction of entering into detailed explanations of why I have rejected the views of others. The footnotes are mainly to point to sources of information for those who wish to follow up my interpretation of particular passages, or to check on matters relating to Hebrew language.

Once more I acknowledge the help given by my wife Mairi, who, along with other assistance, worked with me through the commentary on the text of Amos in our evening devotions. That has been our practice for seven biblical books—Exodus, Deuteronomy, Psalms, Isaiah, Daniel, Joel, and now Amos.

ALLAN M. HARMAN
March 2021

Abbreviations

ANEP — *The Ancient Near East in Pictures*, ed. J. B. Pritchard, 2nd ed. (Princeton: Princeton University Press, 1969).

ANET — *Ancient Near Eastern Texts Relating to the Old Testament*, 3rd ed. (Princeton: Princeton University Press, 1969).

ASV — *American Standard Version.*

AV — *Authorised Version*, or as it is sometimes known, the *King James Version.*

BASOR — *Bulletin of the American Schools of Oriental Research*

BHS[5] — *Biblia Hebraica Stuttgartensia*, 5th ed. (Stuttgart: Deutsche Bibelstiftung, 1997).

BS — *Bibliotheca Sacra.*

c. — Latin, around, about.

CHAL — *A Concise Hebrew and Aramaic Lexicon of the Old Testament* (Grand Rapids: Eerdmans, 1988).

DCH — *Dictionary of Classical Hebrew*, ed. David J. A. Clines, 7 vols. (Sheffield: Sheffield Academic Press, 1993-2011).

DIHG-S — *J. C. L. Gibson, Davidson's Introductory Hebrew Grammar-Syntax*, 4th ed. (Edinburgh: T. & T. Clark, 1994).

DOTT — *Documents from Old Testament Times.*

EBC	*Expositor's Bible Commentary.*
ESV	*English Standard Version* (Wheaton, IL: Crossway, 2001)
Heb	Hebrew.
IBHS	Bruce K. Waltke and M. O'Connor, *An Introduction to Biblical Hebrew Syntax* (Winona Lake: Eisenbrauns, 1990).
IDBSupp	*Interpreter's Dictionary of the Bible Supplement* (Nashville: Abingdon Press, 1976).
ISBE	*International Standard Bible Encyclopaedia*, 4 vols. (Grand Rapids: Eerdmans, 1979).
lit.	literally.
LXX	The Septuagint, the oldest and most important Greek translation of the Old Testament made in Egypt about 250 BC.
mg.	margin.
MT	Massoretic text, the Hebrew text of the Old Testament that became recognised as authoritative after the fall of Jerusalem in 70 AD.
NASB	*New American Standard Bible*: Updated Edition (Anaheim, CA: Foundation Publications, 1997).
NEB	*New English Bible* (New York: Oxford University Press, 1976).
NIDOTTE	*New International Dictionary of Old Testament Theology and Exegesis,* ed. Willem A. VanGemeren, 5 vols. (Grand Rapids: Zondervan, 1997).
NIV	*New International Version* (Colorado Springs: International Bible Society, 1984).
NKJV	*New King James Version* (Nashville: Thomas Nelson, 1982).

NLT	*New Living Translation* (Wheaton: Tyndale House, 1996).
NRSV	*New Revised Standard Version* (Grand Rapids: Zondervan, 1989).
REB	*Revised English Bible* (Oxford: Oxford University Press, 1989).
RSV	*Revised Standard Version* (The Bible Societies, 1952).
RV	*Revised Version* (1881).
TDOT	*Theological Dictionary of the Old Testament*, 15 vols. (Grand Rapids: Eerdmans, 1974-2006).
TWOT	*Theological Wordbook of the Old Testament*, 2 vols. (Chicago: Moody Press, 1980).

Glossary

double-duty	This is the term given to a type of ellipsis where a grammatical form, such as a preposition or suffix present in one member of a parallelism, serves also for the missing form in the other.
fixed pair	The term 'fixed pair' refers to words that regularly occur in parallel expressions in Hebrew, e.g. head//skull, earth//dust, mouth//lip.
hapax legomenon	A word only occurring once.
targum	An Aramaic translation or paraphrase of some part of the Old Testament. They were oral at first but were later written. The earliest examples (from Qumran) are from the 2nd century BC.
theophany	A visible appearance of God.

Notes on Hebrew

Verbal Themes

qal	*Qal*
ni.	*Nif'al*
pi.	*Pi'el*
pu.	*Pu'al*
hi.	*Hif'al*
ho.	*Hof'al*
hitp.	*Hitpa'el*

Grammatical Expressions

absol. inf	Absolute infinitive: a verbal form normally placed before another form of the verb in order to emphasise it.
cognate accusative	The use of a noun as the object of a verb which comes from the same root, e.g., 'They dreaded [with] dread' (Psa. 14:5).
coh.	cohortative: indirect imperative forms in the 1st person singular and plural, e.g., 'Let me (us) send.'
constr.	construct: a noun, usually in a shortened form, placed before another noun and with a close semantic relation to it, covering all the nuances of the English *of.*
imper.	imperative
imperf.	Imperfect, a verbal conjugation in Hebrew that identifies a situation as fluid or in motion.
inf.	infinitive
interrogative marker	The use of h[a] prefixed to a sentence to change it into a question.

juss.	jussive, 3rd person forms of the indirect imperative, e.g., 'Let him (them) send.'
masc.	masculine
part.	participle
pass.	passive
perf.	perfect, a verbal conjugation in Hebrew that identifies a situation as static or at rest.
pers.	person
pl.	plural
s.	singular

Transliteration of Consonants

alef	'
bet	b
gimel	g
dalet	d
he	h
vav	v
zayin	z
chet	ch (as in German *ich*, or Scottish loch)
tet	t
yod	y
kaf	k
lamed	l
mem	m
nun	n
samek	s
ayin	'
peh	p/f
tsadeh	ts
qof	q

resh	r
sin	s
shin	sh
taw	t

Notes

1. Long vowels are marked with a circumflex, e.g., â, ê, î, ô, û.

2. Hebrew words are normally accented on the final syllable. However, there is a group of nouns in which the stress is placed on the first of a pair of vowels, resulting in next-to-last syllable stress. This is marked by the use of an acute, e.g., *régel* (foot).

3. The English version used in this commentary is the *English Standard Version* (Wheaton, IL: Crossway, 2001).

I

Introduction to the Book of Amos

1. *Its Setting*

The prophet Amos was one of a group of God's messengers who ministered to Israel/Judah in the 8th century BC. He and Hosea were near contemporaries who brought God's word to bear on the northern kingdom of Israel, while Isaiah and Micah were directed by God to the southern kingdom of Judah. These prophets are often referred to as 'the writing prophets.' While significant earlier prophets such as Elijah and Elisha had ministered to God's people, their ministry was oral, not written. The only exception to this is the letter Elijah wrote to King Jehoram (2 Chron. 21:12-15).[1] However, in the 8th century BC, prophets started to minister God's word by writing as well as speaking their messages. Hence, though reference is made to Amos' spoken ministry (Amos 7:10, 11), yet he, or someone else, recorded his messages in written text. The prophets, by Jewish tradition, are considered as the writers of the history from Joshua to 2 Kings, and hence the name for this section of the Old Testament is 'the former prophets.' The one prophet who is specifically named as contributing to the written history of Israel and Judah is Isaiah, who wrote of 'the rest of the acts of Hezekiah and his good deeds' (2 Chron. 32:32).

[1] Difficulties surround this letter because of the time gap involved between Elijah's translation and the reception of the letter by Jehoram. For discussion of the problems and a possible solution, see Roy E. Knuteson, 'Elijah's Little-Known Letter in 2 Chronicles 21:12-15,' *BS* 162 (2005), pp. 23-32.

To say that before the 8th century BC the prophets normally brought oral messages from God to the people is not to deny that written records must have existed. Without such records, the sections inserted in the historical books about individual prophets and their message could not have been written. No evidence is available to show whether it was the prophets themselves who wrote down the messages, or others who took on this task. Amos appears to have been the first of sixteen literary prophets, as the internal evidence suggests that his prophecy precedes any of the others.[1]

There are some good reasons why this alteration to written messages took place. The first of these reasons is internationalism. This was a significant period for the development of international relationships, especially through treaties. These treaties were written, and the general populace of a country were included in their scope. If a treaty was broken, a royal messenger was sent to declare the impending judgment or application of the covenantal curses on the rebellious people. The biblical text contains one notable incident concerning a royal messenger and that is the account of the Rabshakeh (an office, not a personal name) who came on Sennacherib's orders to bring a message to king Hezekiah of Judah (2 Kings 18:17–19:19, and the parallel account in Isaiah 36–37). Most probably an official written decree lies behind the Rabshakeh's oral presentation, and this may well have been the pattern: a written document that was then given fuller oral explanation.

The second reason is the increase in popular literacy. Written prophecy, in contrast to oral proclamation, could only take place in the context of the general literacy of the people to whom the prophecies were addressed. The Gezer calendar (10th–9th century BC) is probably, as the script is awkward, a schoolboy's attempt at writing practice, or else from someone whose writing skills were not well

[1] The possibility exists that Jonah son of Amittai was earlier (see 2 Kings 14:25), but the composition of the book called Jonah may have been later.

developed. Many seals, dating from around the 7th century BC, have been found and they only contain the name of the owner, without any pictorial representation. This is evidence that literacy was becoming widespread, and therefore writing could be used both to record prophetic speeches and to distribute them among the general population.

The period of Amos' ministry, somewhere around 760 BC, was in a period of great prosperity for both Israel and Judah, and with none of the tension and turmoil that marked out the concluding years of Israel's existence before the Assyrians took Samaria in 722 BC. Israel was stronger from a military point of view, while it was geographically larger than it had been for a long time. Under Jeroboam II (793–753 BC) the borders of Israel had been pushed out to reclaim territory that had been lost since the death of Solomon. A long period of peace between Israel and Judah enabled both nations to enjoy great prosperity, and the wealth on display in Israel is described by Amos. The existence of very varied housing in Israel has been shown by excavations at Tirzah (the capital before Omri built Samaria), while Amos draws attention to the economic, social and moral conditions. The first of Amos' descriptions of conditions in Israel (2:6-8) summarises the moral delinquency that extended to deceitful commercial transactions, abuse of religious ordinances, and perversion of the legal system.

Like many of the prophets, Amos conveyed his messages in poetry, not prose. Almost all of chapters 1-6 are poetry, though parts of the visions in chapters 7 and the early part of chapter 8 are prose, before poetry is resumed for the remainder of the book. This means that in interpreting this book we have to face two difficulties. The first is that prophecy by its very nature is not pre-written history, and it is therefore harder to interpret. For instance, intervals of time are not given with the same precision as in historical writing, and hence it is often hard to determine precisely the time frame of depicted future events. The second is the fact that it is Hebrew poetry. This adds to the complexity, as many features of Old Testament poetry are different from Western poetry and give an additional layer of difficulty to the interpretative process.[1]

Since Amos and his fellow prophets claimed that they received their messages by revelation, this implies that God's intention was that his word was to be conveyed in a form that had an element of strangeness about it. Poetry immediately proclaims this strangeness by its use of archaic language, asserting the primacy of image, and by a range of other literary devices. Above all else, readers or hearers of poetry experience the content, not just simply listen to an abstract idea. Amos' use of imagery, most of it in warning passages, must have brought home to those of his day, in a very dramatic way, the awful reality of God's judgments. Rather than poetry detracting from the message, the form served to accentuate it.[2]

2. *The Prophet Amos*

While some other Old Testament prophets are known both by their own book and also by references to them in the historical books (e.g., for Isaiah, see 2 Kings 18–20), all that we know about Amos is contained in this book (see the exegesis of 1:1). He claimed that he had been called by the LORD from his work as a farmer to go and assume a prophetic role (see the exegesis of 7:10-17). This accounts for the sneering jibe of Amaziah the priest at Bethel that he should go home and prophesy there (7:12). No account exists of any prophecy issued by Amos in his own country.

His name should not be confused with that of Isaiah's father, Amoz, for the spelling of the two names differs in Hebrew. Amos

[1] I have commented, with some more detail, on both of these issues when discussing the form of prophecy in the book of Isaiah. See *Isaiah: A Covenant to be Kept for the Sake of the Church* (Fearn: Christian Focus Publications, 2011), pp. 22-24.

[2] In addition to other discussions on Hebrew poetry, see especially Leland Ryken, 'Respect for the Principles of Poetry,' in his book *The Word of God in English: Criteria and Excellence in Bible Translation* (Wheaton, IL: Crossway, 2002), pp. 243-56.

was a southerner, from Tekoa in Judah, who was called to go north to Israel and there proclaim God's message. His earlier ministry was clearly oral, since the priest Amaziah referred to what he had been 'saying' about the king, Jeroboam. He was not deterred from carrying out his role as the LORD's messenger because of Amaziah's intervention. No further information is available about his continued ministry in either Israel or Judah, and no speculation adds anything to the evidence we have in the Book of Amos itself. His role is important, though, as it highlights the essential nature of the calling of a prophet. Communal life or instruction within a group of sons of the prophets was not a prerequisite for a prophetic ministry (see Amos' denial of this background, 7:14). What mattered was God's call, and often prophets appeared on the scene without any forewarning (see the way in which Elijah is suddenly introduced in 1 Kings 17:1).

3. *The Theology of Amos*

The central themes of Amos are similar to the other 8th-century BC prophets (Hosea, Isaiah and Micah), though each of them has distinctive features. This is not surprising, as along with common teaching, they all dealt with specific issues that related to their own ministry. In particular, the themes that Amos' contemporary Hosea discoursed about must be considered in parallel with his theology, as clearly both were directed to deal with covenantal disobedience by Israel. Moreover, they were acting as guardians of the theocracy, seeking to hold kings and other leaders accountable to God for their actions. In relation to the bond with the LORD they were 'covenant enforcement mediators,'[1] and thus in fellowship with their LORD.

[1] The phrase, 'guardians of the theocracy' follows on from the phrase used by the evangelical German writer, Gustav Oehler, in the 19th century, who wrote of the prophets as 'the watchmen of the theocracy.' The second phrase, 'covenant enforcement mediators,' comes from Douglas Stuart in his discussion on the prophets in Gordon D. Fee and Douglas Stuart, *How to Read the Bible for All Its Worth: A Guide to Understanding the Bible*, 3rd ed. (Grand Rapids: Zondervan, 2003), pp. 184-86.

The message of these prophets, including Amos, can be summarised under four headings, all of which relate to the covenant.[1]

a. The God of the Covenant

At the heart of the prophetic ministry was the nature of Israel's God. The prophets were setting forth declarations that claimed to come from the God who had redeemed Israel from bondage in Egypt, and who had entered graciously into a covenant with his special possession (Exod. 19:5; Psa. 135:4). One way to look at their conception of God is to examine the various titles they ascribe to him. Here are those used in Amos:

> the LORD (*yhwh*, 47 times)
> the LORD your God (*yhwh ᵉloheḳâ*, 1 time)
> the Lord GOD (*ᵃdonay yhwh*, 19 times)
> the LORD, the God of hosts (*yhwh ᵉlohê [hats]tsᵉvâ'ôt*, 6 times)
> the Lord GOD, the God of hosts (*'adonay yhwh ᵉlohê hatstsᵉvâ'ôt*, 1 time)
> the LORD, the God of hosts, the Lord (*yhwh ᵉlohê hatstsᵉvâ'ôt ᵃdonay*, 1 time)

Most common is the simple covenantal designation, LORD (*yhwh*), but all the other compound expressions include it. From the time that Moses met with God at the burning bush (Exod. 3:1-14), the name 'the LORD' (*yhwh*) was the dominant one for Israel's God, even though it had been known and used earlier. It was his covenantal name, and, coming from the Hebrew verb 'to be, to exist' (*hâyâh*), it probably denoted God as the one who had life in himself and who was also the lifegiver.[2] Amos' use of it is similar to his fellow

[1] I am here basically following the pattern set out by Geerhardus Vos, *Biblical Theology* (Edinburgh: Banner of Truth Trust, 1975), pp. 234-96.

[2] I have discussed further the name 'the LORD' (*yhwh*) in my commentary *Exodus: God's Kingdom of Priests* (Fearn: Christian Focus Publications, 2017), pp. 34, 71-73.

8th-century prophets, and this points to his understanding of God as the covenantal God whom he had to represent to Israel.

Like other prophets, Amos directs his audience's attention to the LORD's power displayed in his creative and providential work (4:13; 5:8, 9), but more particularly to his redemptive work. He brought Israel up out of Egypt (2:10; 3:1; 9:7), and led them into the land of promise (2:10). He was the God of history, noted for his acts against those who disobeyed him (4:10, 11) and who threatened divine action against his enemies, to be seen especially in his coming judgments on Israel's neighbours (1:4, 5, 7, 8, 10, 12, 14, 15; 2:2, 3) and even on Israel herself (1:13-16; 3:11, 14, 15).

The threats against Israel become more specific as the prophetic voice continues its message. Early warnings are of disaster in the city (3:6), and of the need of the people to prepare to meet their God (4:12). Then come declarations about Gilgal going into captivity (5:5), with the specification that exile is going to be 'beyond Damascus' (5:27). The certainty of exile is repeated several times (6:7, 14; 7:17; 9:4, 9). This message was a continuation of the covenantal curses (Lev. 26:32-35; Deut. 28:36, 37, 64-68). What was going to happen to Israel in 722 BC, and to Judah in 586 BC, would bring the same definitive statement of guilt: 'It is because they abandoned the covenant of the LORD, the God of their fathers, which he made with them when he brought them out of the land of Egypt' (Deut. 29:25).

Another aspect of God's nature and power was the extent of his control over other nations as well. It was not just Israel and Judah who came under his oversight, but various other nations as well. This comes out at the beginning of the prophecy with the oracles against the surrounding nations—Damascus, Gaza, Tyre, Edom, Ammon, and Moab (1:2–2:3). Later passages extend that rule over Egypt (4:10), also to the Philistines and Arameans (9:7).

b. The Covenantal Relationship

Though the covenantal theme is pervasive in the Old Testament, it has often been noted how infrequently the actual word 'covenant' (*b^e^rît*) occurs in the Psalter and in the prophetical books. This is true also of the book of Amos, yet the whole concept of covenant underlies the message. We have to reckon with an extensive vocabulary in the Old Testament both for descriptive terms that point to the covenant itself, and also terms that are more closely connected with stipulations or with relationships that are established by a covenant. A variety of expressions can be used for covenantal commitment, for the relationship established, and for the making and breaking of solemn oaths. A cluster of terms can occur in a single context. Israel was a people who were brought up out of the land of Egypt (2:10; 3:1). She had been brought through the desert, and by God's power had overcome the Amorites and occupied their land (2:9, 10). All the geographical references assume that Israel was God's covenantal nation from the time of the exodus.

This point is crystallised by the words at the opening of chapter 3. It is spoken against 'the whole family' whom God brought up out of Egypt: 'You only have I known of all the families of the earth' (3:2). This is a verb that is often used in covenantal contexts when speaking of the relationship between God and Israel (see Gen. 18:19 and 2 Sam. 7:20). In the Near Eastern treaties 'to know' is used of a suzerain's recognition of a vassal's relationship to him. Hence, its appearance in Amos 3:2 is a significant use of a covenantal term.

c. The Breach of the Covenant

The first message against Israel (2:6-16) reminded the people how unthankful they had been to their covenantal overlord. He redeemed them from Egypt, destroyed enemies before them, and gave them prophets (2:10, 11). But, in spite of God's grace to them, their manner of life contradicted what covenantal obedience should be (2:6-8; 5:7, 11, 12; 6:1-6; 8:5, 6). Instead of continuing to seek evil, they should have been seeking good (5:14). The society in Amos' day was marked by maladministration and various injustices, and so he charges them with breaching their covenantal requirements.

In challenging Judah with her sin, Amos specifically says she had 'rejected' (*mâ'as*) the law of the LORD and failed to keep his decrees (2:4). The use of the verb 'reject' is significant, for it is also used in various covenantal contexts. In Leviticus 26:15 rejection of the LORD's decrees is tantamount to covenantal violation, and as such would merit expulsion from the land (Lev. 26:43). For example, Israel's action in asking for a king was a rejection of God (1 Sam. 8:7), while Saul's rejection of God resulted in his own rejection by him (1 Sam. 15:26). Amos is therefore charging his own nation, Judah, with serious violation of the covenant.

Divine provision had been made for revelation to come to Israel, not by means of Canaanite mediums, but by prophets who would be raised up from among the people (Deut. 18:9-16). The people of Israel were reminded of this by Amos (2:11), but his accusation was that they had instructed the prophets not to prophesy (2:12). Once the people had made up their minds to go their own way, they did not wish to hear any further from God's messengers. Similarly, they despised God's institution of the Nazirites, and perverted that provision by making them drink wine (2:11, 12).

The references to worship that Amos makes are important. Clearly many aspects of covenantal life were being observed, but the people had externalised the stipulations, and perfunctory adherence to them had taken the place of heartfelt religious devotion and actions. The nature of the covenant should have been a warning to them, but instead it bolstered their feelings of self-confidence and pride.

In spite of the people's sin, mercy was still held out to Israel. The people were encouraged to seek the LORD and live (5:4, 5).

The warnings in the Pentateuch concerning the consequences of forsaking the LORD also contained promises of gracious restoration following confession and repentance (Lev. 26:40-45).

d. Covenantal Eschatology

The threat of exile that Amos gives for disobedient Israel would far surpass any previous judgments of God. Amos warns that invasion would bring tremendous distress on the population (see 3:11, 12; 4:1-3; 5:3, 16), but that something even more disastrous was ahead. While the populace might know about the coming day of the LORD, they mistakenly thought that it was going to be a glorious day for Israel. Instead, it was going to be a day of darkness and distress (see the exegesis of 5:18-27). At this stage in Israel's history the day of the LORD was pictured in terms of judgment in the immediate future, not judgment at some undesignated time far ahead.

Amongst all the gloomy prophecy, three aspects of Amos' message gave hope. The first was the way in which Israel was addressed. In spite of all her sin, the LORD still addressed her as '*my people Israel*' (7:8, 15; 8:2). The counterfoil to this is the declaration that closes the book: 'says *the LORD your God*' (9:15). Here in summary is the central core of the covenant. God took Israel to be his people, while he promised that he was her God. In spite of all that had happened, Israel was still God's people. To use the analogy that was employed a little later by the prophet Isaiah, Israel was the wife who was separated but not divorced (Isa. 50:1; 54:6-8). Israel and Judah together were 'the whole family' that the LORD brought up out of Egypt (3:1). Though divided at the time of Amos' ministry, in later prophecy at the time of the exile it was made clear that when the return to Palestine took place the division would disappear and Israel and Judah would indeed be one (Ezek. 37:15-23).

The second aspect of hope is the promise of restoration for David's fallen tent (see the exegesis of 9:11, 12). While not spelt out in any detail, indications of hope for the Davidic family must have been a strong note of encouragement. Over against the difficulties facing Israel in the time of Amos' ministry, the picture is presented of restoration, and that was to include possession of Gentile nations (see the use that James made of this passage at the council in Jerusalem, Acts 15:13-21).

The third element of hope is in the concluding verses of the prophecy (9:14, 15). The promise there is that a return to Palestine will take place, initiated by God himself ('*I* will restore the fortunes of my people Israel; '*I* will plant them on their land'). The result of the return is stated in idyllic terms, with vineyards and gardens yielding abundant produce for the returnees. The same message to Israel was proclaimed by Hosea in similar language (Hos. 14:5-8).

4. *The Structure of the Book of Amos*

Compared with some other prophetical books of the Old Testament, the basic structure of Amos is not difficult to ascertain. The first two chapters consist of oracles against six neighbouring political entities (Syria, Gaza, Tyre, Edom, Ammon, and Moab; 1:1–2:3), and then against both Judah and Israel (2:4-16). The preliminary oracle against Israel is developed by means of three proclamations in 3:1–6:14, all beginning with the call to hear the word of the LORD (3:1; 4:1; 5:1). Then follow five visions of coming judgment (7:1–9:10), with the final section in the prophecy pointing to days of blessing when the Davidic family will be reinvigorated and Israel brought back from exile (9:11-15). The link between some sub-sections may differ from commentary to commentary but the general pattern is universally acknowledged. The structure of Amos is then as follows:

Part 1: ***Amos and His Message (1:1–2:16)***

1. Superscription (1:1)
2. Introduction to Amos' Message: The Theme (1:2)
3. Judgment on the Nations (1:3–2:16)
   a. Damascus (1:3-5)
   b. Gaza (1:6-8)
   c. Tyre (1:9, 10)
   d. Edom (1:11, 12)
   e. Ammon (1:13-15)
   f. Moab (2:1-3)
   g. Judah (2:4, 5)
   h. Israel (2:6-16)

Part 2: ***Oracles against the Chosen People (3:1–5:17)***

1. Breach of the Covenant (3:1-15)
   a. God's Punishment Announced (3:1, 2)
   b. Penetrating Questions (3:3-6)
   c. The Disclosure of God's Will (3:7, 8)
   d. Just Punishment (3:9-15)

2. Failure to Repent (4:1-13)
   a. Condemnation of Socialites (4:1-3)
   b. Sinful Worship (4:4, 5)
   c. Lessons Forgotten (4:6-9)
   d. Failure to Repent (4:10, 11)
   e. A Meeting with God (4:12, 13)

3. Indictment of an Unjust People (5:1-17)
   a. Lament over Israel (5:1-3)
   b. A Call to Repentance (5:4-6)
   c. The Reasons for God's Judgment on Israel (5:7-13)

d. Encouragement to Live (5:14, 15)
e. Prosperity Lost (5:16, 17)

Part 3: ***Announcement of the Exile (5:18–6:14)***

1. Unexpected Judgment (5:18-20)
2. False Worship and its Consequences (5:21-27)
3. Declaration against those Living in Luxury (6:1-7)
4. Judgment against Pride (6:8-14)

Part 4: ***Visions of Judgment (7:1–9:10)***

1. The First Vision—A Plague of Locusts (7:1-3)
2. The Second Vision—Fire (7:4-6)
3. The Third Vision—The Wall (7:7-9)
4. Interaction among Prophet, Priest, and King (7:10-17)
5. The Fourth Vision—A Basket of Summer Fruits (8:1-3)
6. Declarations against Greedy Merchants (8:4-6)
7. The LORD's Oath against the Greedy Merchants (8:7-10)
8. The Threat of Famine (8:11-14)
9. The Fifth Vision—The LORD in His Glory (9:1-4)
10. A Doxology Proclaiming the LORD's Might (9:5, 6)
11. The Continuation of the Judgment Theme (9:7-10)

Part 5: ***Epilogue: Eventual Restoration (9:11-15)***

1. Restoration of the Davidic Dynasty (9:11, 12)
2. Restoration of Israel (9:13-15)

2

Amos and His Message (1:1–2:16)

1. *Superscription (1:1)*

> 1. *The words of Amos, who was among the shepherds of Tekoa, which he saw concerning Israel in the days of Uzziah king of Judah and in the days of Jeroboam the son of Joash, king of Israel, two years before the earthquake.*

The book begins with a declaration that it contains the words of Amos (*'âmôs*), a shepherd from Tekoa, a form of introduction used also by Jeremiah (1:1). No one else in the Old Testament bears the name Amos. It is probably a shortened form of Amasiah (*'amâsyâ*, 2 Chron. 17:16), and it means 'sustained by the LORD.'[1] This is repeated in 7:14, where additional information is given. Amos had been a breeder of cattle and a herdsman looking after small animals.[2] The description of him as a shepherd (*noqêd*) does not use the usual Hebrew word (*ro'eh*), but there does not seem any doubt as to the meaning as he calls himself a herdsman (*bôqêr*, 7:14). He also cared for sycamore-fig trees, and, though not coming from a family of prophets, was called by God to the work of prophecy. These descriptive terms concerning

[1] A seal from Amman carries the name *'ms'l* showing that the same root could be combined with other divine names.

[2] The word used is *ts'on*, which can denote both sheep and goats.

Amos may denote a significant farmer, for Mesha, king of Moab, is also called a 'shepherd' (*noqêd*) in 2 Kings 3:4. However, there is insufficient evidence to be certain as to Amos' wealth or social position.

Tekoa was situated about 16 km (10 miles) south-east of Jerusalem, and was a fortified town in the period after the division of the kingdom (2 Chron. 11:6). It was in the southern kingdom of Judah, yet the message of Amos was directed to the northern kingdom of Israel. Later this led to the taunt of Amaziah to him: 'go, flee away to the land of Judah' (7:12).

The description of how the message was communicated to him uses the verb 'saw' (*châzâh*), which is an indication of divine revelation. This same verb is used at the commencement of other prophecies (e.g. Isa. 1:1; Mic. 1:1; Hab. 1:1). The reception of this revelation is placed within the reigns of Uzziah in the south (Judah) and of Jeroboam II in the north (Israel). This was, in general, a period of stability for both kingdoms because of the long reigns of Uzziah (792–740 BC) and Jeroboam II (793–753 BC). Their reigns overlapped during the period 767–753 BC. The time is given as 'two years before the earthquake.' An earthquake that hit Hazor has been placed between 765 and 760 BC. This dating is therefore appropriate for the period of Amos' ministry.

2. *Introduction to Amos' Message: The Theme (1:2)*

> 2. *And he said: 'The* Lord *roars from Zion and utters his voice from Jerusalem; the pastures of the shepherds mourn, and the top of Carmel withers.'*

Several of the Old Testament prophets depict the Lord roaring in judgment (Isa. 31:4; Jer. 2:30; Hos. 5:14), and Amos does here (and in 3:4, 8) to indicate that a divine visitation is to take place on Israel. Like a lion roaring before it attacks, the Lord was giving his warnings from

Zion, thundering from Jerusalem.[1] The language here is identical to that in Joel 3:16. Rather than Jerusalem and Zion being places of safety, they are where the judgments originate. This too should have been a further indication to the people of Israel that none of the false sanctuaries in the land could replace the true sanctuary in Jerusalem. The use of the divine name, the LORD (*yhwh*), is significant. The covenantal name of God was a reminder that though the northern tribes were rebellious and idolatrous, God had not cast them off.

The lion's roar has implications for the land as well as the people. The pastures are affected, while the notable landmark of Israel, Carmel, loses its lush vegetation as it 'withers.' This is a pertinent reminder of God's sovereignty over the people and their land. His concern for Israel will be shown by the fact that the northern tribes are the intended destination of Amos and his message. Judgment is announced, but it could be averted. The book, which commences with a note of warning, ends with gracious promises (9:13-15).

Application

> The interaction of kings and prophets in Israel was important. While both offices had been announced much earlier in Israel's history, they both came to prominence at the same time. When God permitted his people to have a king (1 Sam. 8-10), he also brought the role of prophets to the fore so they could guard the theocratic kingdom. They were not originators of a new message, but heralds of the covenantal law that had been given through Moses. Even in the last book of the Old Testament the LORD calls for adherence to 'the law of my servant Moses, the statutes and rules that I commanded him at Horeb for all Israel' (Mal. 4:4). Both prophets and kings were a gracious provision by God for his people, and also pointed

[1] The Hebrew idiom, *yittên qôlô*, 'gives his voice,' is rightly taken by the ESV to indicate thunder.

them ahead to the one who would speak God's final word, and who would rule with perfect justice.

3. *Judgment on the Nations (1:3–2:16)*

Before each of the oracles in this section of Amos is considered, some comment on the phenomenon of prophetic oracles against the nations is needed.

1. Amos and his fellow 8th-century BC prophet Isaiah both directed messages to the nations, as did the later prophets Jeremiah and Ezekiel. The passages in question are:[1]

> Amos 1:3–2:16;
> Isaiah 13:1–23:18;
> Jeremiah 46:1–51:58;
> Ezekiel 25:1–32:32.

The fact that the prophets included these messages shows that they had a vision that went far beyond Israel/Judah. They knew that the LORD was sovereign over the nations.

2. The prophet's choice of nations depended on which were important neighbours, and which were a direct threat to the people of God. This explains why Amos has no oracle against Egypt or Babylon, in contrast to Isaiah, Jeremiah and Ezekiel.

3. Nothing in the text itself explains the order in which the nations are addressed. Various explanations have been given.[2] Most probably some geographical arrangement has been utilised. A criss-crossing order seems too difficult, as does a spiral arrangement,[3] though this suggestion does place correct emphasis on the climax of the accusations coming against Israel.

[1] A very useful chart listing the messages against the foreign nations can be found in Lamar Cooper, Sr., *Ezekiel* (NAC: Broadman & Holman, 1994), p. 244.

[2] For a good summary discussion, see Thomas J. Finley, *Joel, Amos, Obadiah* (Wycliffe Exegetical Commentary: Chicago: Moody Press, 1990), pp. 134-36.

[3] See the one given by William Hendriksen, *A Survey of the Bible*, 4th ed. (Grand Rapids: Baker Book House, 1976), p. 231.

4. The primary purpose of these oracles was with the people of Israel/Judah. No evidence exists that the prophets actually went and proclaimed these messages in person to those addressed. It is clear that the intention was to direct messages to God's people, and this becomes very apparent when Amos, after addressing the most distant of the nations on his list (e.g., Damascus), gradually comes closer home and indicts Judah and Israel for their sins.

5. In Amos the oracles against the nations take on a standardised form:

> *This is what the* LORD *says:*
> *For three sins of [the nation] even for four, I will not turn back my wrath.*
> *Because [with description of the sins committed]*
> *I will send fire upon [the nation]*
> *says the [Sovereign]* LORD.

The final declaration is omitted in the oracle against Tyre, Edom and Judah, while the oracle against Israel concludes with the synonymous expression, 'declares the LORD' (*n^{e}'um yhwh*).

6. The crimes of all these nations have something in common: they are all crimes of atrocity, such as threshing Gilead with implements of sharp iron, or burning the bones of the king of Edom with lime. These nations were violating all humanitarian rights. The fact that Israel/Judah had God's law made their sins all the more serious in his sight. Privilege could not be cited as a claim for mercy. The fact that Israel was in such a special relationship with God meant that judgment for her sins was all the more certain and terrible.

a. Damascus (1:3-5)

3, 4. *Thus says the* LORD: *'For three transgressions of Damascus, and for four, I will not revoke the punishment, because they have threshed Gilead with threshing sledges of iron. So I will send a fire upon the house of Hazael, and it shall devour the strongholds of Ben-hadad.'*

The oracles open with a declaration, 'Thus says the LORD,' that is frequent in the Old Testament and which is used to introduce prophetic messages of judgment as well as those of salvation (see its use in Jer. 47:2; 48:1; Ezek. 25:3 along with this passage). It is a preface to an authoritative declaration that relates to sin. The Hebrew word is 'transgression' (*pésha'*), a term that most often in the Old Testament denotes rebellion against the LORD, Israel's suzerain. The phrase 'For three transgressions of Damascus, and for four, I will not revoke the punishment,' occurs seven more times in chapters 1 and 2, substituting each time the name of the recipient of the message. This is an idiomatic Hebrew and Semitic phrase that is an example of number parallelism. Because a number cannot have a parallel, the next higher digit is used, and the whole expression simply means 'sin upon sin, many sins.'[1] The Hebrew text literally says, 'I will not turn it back,' without defining what 'it' means. In the contexts in chapters 1 and 2, it seems that the reference is to God's wrath demonstrated in judgment.

Damascus is in view, the royal city of the Syrians (in Heb. *'ᵃrâm*) whom David had subdued. In Solomon's time, the Syrians regained their independence under Rezon (1 Kings 11:23-25). Repeated attacks against Israel followed, and Syria's cruelty was great because 'they have threshed Gilead with threshing sledges of iron.' Gilead was the area in Transjordania nearest to the Jordan River and between the Arnon and Jabbok rivers. In spite of its natural resources and beauty it often faced difficulties and dangers. The threshing sledges referred to were not used for threshing grain, but seemingly used as an extremely cruel torture against captives. David used 'sharp iron instruments' against the Ammonites (2 Sam. 12:31), so similar

[1] For discussion of the idiom, see W. G. E. Watson, *Classical Hebrew Poetry: A Guide to Its Techniques* (Sheffield: JSOT, 1984), pp. 144-49.

practices were well known to Israel and Judah. That too would have provoked feelings of fear in those hearing Amos' messages.

The threat is that fire will be sent 'upon the house of Hazael,' and the result will be the destruction of the fortresses of Ben-hadad. It is the LORD himself who is going to execute judgment, and this statement occurs as a refrain in each of the oracles, except for the final one (2:6-16), though in 1:14 the verb is 'kindle' (*hitstsatî*), not 'send' (*shillachtî*). The change does not make any real difference to the meaning. The same threat of sending fire also occurs, in addition to the ones in chapters 1 and 2, in Hosea 8:14 and Ezekiel 39:6. Fire was often used as a weapon of destruction during warfare (see 2 Kings 8:12 and 25:9), and hence could well serve as a description of the LORD's actions in taking recompense.

It is unclear whether 'the house of Hazael' refers to the individual king, or to the dynasty. If it is to the individual, the reference is the king whom Elisha was commanded to anoint (2 Kings 8:7-15), and who usurped the throne by murdering Ben-hadad (2 Kings 8:15). However, it could be a reference to later kings who followed. *Ben-hadad* may well have been a throne name of the Syrian kings, as *Pharaoh* was for the Egyptian rulers. The threat is directed against the royal palaces.

> 5. *'I will break the gate-bar of Damascus, and cut off the inhabitants from the Valley of Aven, and him who holds the scepter from Beth-eden; and the people of Syria shall go into exile to Kir,' says the LORD.*

The threat also involved the city of Damascus. A gate-bar (*b^eriach*) was used as a security measure on city gates, though little is known about how it was attached. In other passages, the breaking or burning of bars clearly amounts to invasion and destruction (see Isa. 45:2; Lam. 2:9; Nah. 3:13). So it does here. The attack is also to be directed against an individual, (literally) 'the one who sits [on the throne] in the Valley of Aven.' This is not Beth Aven in Israel, which was probably near Bethel (see the reference to it in Josh 7:2; 18:12, and 1 Sam. 13:5; 14:23). It has to be another place of the same name but situated within Syrian territory. Of the suggested locations, perhaps Baalbek in northern Lebanon is the best identification (the ancient Heliopolis). The translation, '*from* the Valley of Aven' also obscures the fact that the verb 'sits' (*yôshêv*) appears elsewhere in the Old Testament as an expression for reigning as king (see Psa. 2:4; 22:3 [Heb. 4]; Isa 10:13). It is a description of the one who rules *in* the Valley of Aven. This is confirmed by the use of the parallel expression 'and him who holds the scepter from Beth-eden.' The same expression ('the one who holds the scepter') is used in verse 8, where again it denotes kingly rule in Philistia. It is used similarly of Babylon in Isaiah 14:5, and of Egypt in Zechariah 10:11. Beth-eden is probably a synonym for Damascus. It cannot escape punishment, and its destiny will be deportation to Kir. The Aramaeans originally came from Kir (Amos 9:7) and to it they were returned. Its location is unknown. At the bidding of King Ahaz the Assyrians came against Damascus, and after capturing it took captives to Kir (2 Kings 16:9). The final, 'says the LORD,' adds confirmation to the opening in verse 3, 'Thus says the LORD.' The oracle begins and ends with declarations regarding its source. The message comes through the prophet Amos, but its origin is with God.

b. Gaza (1:6-8)

> *Thus says the LORD: 'For three transgressions of Gaza, and for four, I will not revoke the punishment, because they carried into exile a whole people to deliver them up to Edom. So I will send a fire upon the wall of Gaza, and it shall devour her strongholds. I will cut off the inhabitants from Ashdod, and him who holds the scepter from Ashkelon; I will turn my hand against Ekron, and the remnant of the Philistines shall perish,' says the Lord GOD.*

The same formal opening as in the case of Damascus commences the oracle against Gaza. It was a large city in south-west Palestine, occupying a ground area of 55 hectares, and was situated 5 km (3 miles) inland from the Mediterranean Sea. Strongly fortified, ancient Gaza was a major centre on the route from Egypt to the Levant, and was most probably the chief centre of the Philistines.

The Philistines had migrated from Caphtor (probably Crete; see Amos 9:7; Deut. 2:23; Jer. 47:4) some time before the arrival of Israel into Canaan. They were a thorn in the side of Israel for centuries. Because of their power, the tribe of Dan had to seek new territory in the north (Judg. 18). The Philistines had a monopoly on iron, and hence they were able to control both the weaponry and the agricultural implements of Israel (1 Sam. 13:19-21).

The prominent position of Gaza explains why it is first mentioned. Its sin that is highlighted concerns human trade—inhabitants of southern Judah who were shipped off to Edom. Traffic in prisoners was widespread in the Ancient Near East (see verse 9). Ezekiel 27:13 and Joel 3:6 refer to Tyre as being involved in sale of prisoners. Certainly the Tyrians were great traders in general, and selling slaves was just another aspect of their commercial practices.

> 7. *'So I will send a fire upon the wall of Gaza, and it shall devour her strongholds.'*

The declaration of impending judgment on Gaza is pronounced in almost identical terms with the punishment of Damascus that was just given in 1:4. Destructive fire is to be unleashed against the fortified walls of the city. This expression seems to bear overtones of holy war imagery, for the LORD is depicted as carrying out his vengeance on the sinful city.

> 8. *'I will cut off the inhabitants from Ashdod, and him who holds the scepter from Ashkelon; I will turn my hand against Ekron, and the remnant of the Philistines shall perish,' says the Lord GOD.*

Three other Philistine cities in addition to Gaza—Ashdod, Ashkelon and Ekron—are named as representatives of the wider regional grouping. The fifth Philistine city, Gath, may have already been destroyed by Uzziah of Jerusalem, who won extensive victories in the south and south-west during his reign (2 Chron. 26:6).[1] The prophecy says that the divine judgment will encompass the whole Philistine territory until all are consumed, so that not even a remnant will be left. This theme of the remnant is taken up five times in Amos (1:8; 5:3 twice; 5:15; 9:12). Here it is used to stress the severity of punishment that is coming, so that the negative aspect of the proclamation is at the forefront. The expression 'turn my hand against' (Heb. *hêshîv yâd 'al*) is an idiomatic way of stating that power is brought to bear upon someone. Power against Ekron will be 'unleashed' (NASB). The message ends with the use of a double name for God, 'says the Lord GOD' (Heb. *'âmar 'ᵃdonây yhwh*). This combination of *'ᵃdonây* (Lord) with *yhwh*, the tetragrammaton (LORD), occurs over three hundred times in the Hebrew Old Testament. Many versions use 'Lord GOD' for this combination (ESV), whereas the NIV translators opted for 'Sovereign LORD.'

c. Tyre (1:9, 10)

> 9, 10. *Thus says the LORD: 'For three transgressions of Tyre, and for four, I will not revoke the punishment, because they delivered up a whole people to Edom, and did not remember the covenant of brotherhood. So I will send a fire upon the wall of Tyre, and it shall devour her strongholds.'*

9. Attention turns to the significant trading centre of Tyre. The Greek historian Herodotus mentioned that Tyre dated back to at least 2750 BC. It was probably the greatest of the Phoenician city states. It had two harbours, one on an island and the other on the

[1] For details on the Philistines, see *NIDOTTE*, 3, pp. 631-35.

coast. These were linked when a causeway was built by Hiram I (969–936 BC) joining the two together. Over the course of history Tyre was conquered on many occasions. Greek and Roman ruins are accessible on the south side of the old island-city. The remains of a crusader cathedral are nearby, while inland, extensive Roman roads and an incomplete hippodrome are readily accessible.

The opening formula, 'Thus says the LORD,' again serves to introduce an announcement by Amos of divine intention. This is followed by the threat that God's hand will not be turned away from executing punishment. The sin of Tyre was very similar to the sin of Gaza. She took whole communities captive, and then transferred them into Edomite control. The verb used can apply to turning an escaped slave back into the hands of their owner (see Deut. 23:15; 1 Sam. 30:15), or of handing over a fugitive to pursuers (Josh. 20:5). As with the case of Gaza, no actual historical event can be postulated for this action.

The sin of Tyre, though, is even greater than that of Gaza, because the people there disregarded 'a covenant of brotherhood' (Heb., 'and they did not remember a treaty of brothers'). A formal relationship existed between Tyre and the Davidic/Solomonic kingdom of Israel. When Solomon became king, Hiram of Tyre sent him a letter in which he referred to the friendly relationship that had existed between himself and David (1 Kings 5:1 [Heb. 1 Kings 5:15]).[1] It is unclear whether a formal treaty was entered into during David's reign, but the biblical text is explicit that Hiram and Solomon were bound by one (1 Kings 5:12). Just as Hiram had provided material for building the royal palace in Jerusalem (2 Sam. 5:11), so he did for the building of the temple (1 Kings 5:1-12). Preparation of stone and timber for the temple was done jointly by Hiram and Solomon's men and those from Gebal (better known by its modern names of Byblos or Jebail). In return, Solomon provided food for Tyre (2 Chron.

[1] The Heb. verb *'âhav*, 'to love,' is used here in the sense of being a friend. For other examples, see *DCH*, I, p. 138.

2:15) and also ceded certain territory (1 Kings 9:10-14). However, all past relationships between Israel and Tyre were disregarded at some point, and 'whole people' were transferred to Edom.

10. As with Damascus and Gaza, the judgment will be destruction by fire. Tyre was noted for its defences and boasted about her seemingly impregnable position (Ezek. 26:1–28:19). The fall of Tyre was not going to be accomplished by human agency, but by the LORD of hosts, as Isaiah prophesied (Isa. 23:8, 9). This oracle against Tyre lacks the rounding formula, 'says the LORD.'

Application

God not only dealt favourably with Israel but also intervened in history to punish those who had attacked her. Among them were the subjects of these first three oracles. The nation of Syria, and especially its capital Damascus, had shown its hostility towards Israel, though for a time Jeroboam II (780–753 BC) had ruled over Damascus. Later, during Isaiah's ministry, Syria forged an alliance with Israel against Judah (Isa. 7:1, 2; 2 Kings 16:5, 6), but that plan was thwarted by God's sovereign intervention. Man may propose, but it is God's prerogative to dispose. He steps in to protect his people, so that his church is preserved.

Crowns and thrones may perish,
Kingdoms rise and wane,
But the church of Jesus
Ever shall remain.

Sabine Baring-Gould (1834–1924),
'Onward, Christian Soldiers.'

Many in Israel did not recognise that the continued presence of hostile Philistines was due to Israel's own unbelief. Change of leadership, even to kingship, was not going to solve the problem. It was God alone who could promise the ultimate destruction of the Philistines, and that would be achieved through his power. This prophetic oracle (Amos 1:6-8) points to the utter destruction to come on the Philistines.

The third major neighbour close to Israel was Tyre. At times it was of assistance, but its power was exercised in its own interests, not those of God's people. Together with Syria and the Philistine cities, it formed a hedge around Israel that could only be broken by divine intervention. Israel in the days of Amos had to rely upon assurances of God's protecting care and his ability to destroy all ungodly forces arrayed against her. Believers have still to rest on God's promises that he will deal with their oppressors, and the final outcome will be that every knee will bow before the Lord Jesus (Phil. 2:9, 10; Rev. 5:13).

d. Edom (1:11, 12)

11, 12. *Thus says the* L*ORD*: *'For three transgressions of Edom, and for four, I will not revoke the punishment, because he pursued his brother with the sword and cast off all pity, and his anger tore perpetually, and he kept his wrath forever. So I will send a fire upon Teman, and it shall devour the strongholds of Bozrah.'*

11. Attention now turns to countries that were descended from the line of Abraham. The first of these is Edom. When Moses spoke to the assembled Israel prior to leaving Horeb, he reminded them that the Edomites were 'your brothers, the people of Esau' (Deut. 2:4). In the earlier parts of the Old Testament there was comparative friendliness towards Edom (see also Deut. 23:7, 8). However, later books show hostility, with curses being invoked against her (Obad. 1-21; Jer. 49:7-22; Mal. 1:2-5). Here, Amos' message is one of judgment, not blessing.

The opening phrase again emphasises the origin of Amos' message. It is the LORD who speaks. The reason for impending judgment is 'because he pursued his brother with the sword.' The prophecy of Obadiah is directed to Edom, and one of the major sins was the violence that was shown to his brother Jacob, i.e., against the southern kingdom of Judah (Obad. 10-12). The twice repeated 'your brother' in Obadiah points to the grievous nature of the attacks upon Judah. It was with murderous intent that the Edomites pursued Judah 'with the sword.' Instead of blood links with them inspiring kindly actions, the Edomites suppressed any feelings of compassion. Instead they let their continuous anger ('tore perpetually') display itself against their blood brother.

12. As with each of the preceding messages, this one concludes with the threat of fire. The LORD promises to send devouring fire against Teman and against Bozrah. Neither location can be identified today with absolute certainty. Teman was the name of a grandson of Esau (Gen. 36:11; 1 Chron. 1:36), and possibly he gave his name to a district in northern Edom. Other prophets joined with Amos in depicting the destruction of Teman by the LORD (Jer. 49:20; Ezek. 25:13; Obad. 9). Bozrah has been identified with Buseirah, about 48 km (30 miles) south-east of the Dead Sea. The two places are linked together here, suggesting either that they were in close proximity to one another, or that they were essentially the same geographical area.

e. Ammon (1:13-15)

> 13-15. *Thus says the LORD: 'For three transgressions of the Ammonites, and for four, I will not revoke the punishment, because they have ripped open pregnant women in Gilead, that they might enlarge their border. So I will kindle a fire in the wall of Rabbah, and it shall devour her strongholds, with shouting on the day of battle, with a tempest in the day of the whirlwind; and their king shall go into exile, he and his princes together,' says the LORD.*

13. The second of the messages to descendants of Abraham is addressed to the Ammonites. They were the descendants of Lot by Ben-ammi, his son, by incestuous union with his daughter (Gen. 19:38). Israel was told not to provoke them as they came out of Egypt and headed for the land of Canaan (Deut. 2:19). The territory they occupied had been allotted to them by God. Deuteronomy explains that the discrimination against the Ammonites, in that they could not come into the assembly of God's people, was because they had failed to provide for the Israelites on their journey, and because they supported the Moabites in hiring Balaam to pronounce curses against Israel (Deut. 23:3, 4). The Ammonite kingdom was centred on Rabbah, present day Amman, the capital of Jordan.

The message opens with the formula, 'For three transgressions of the Ammonites, and for four, I will not revoke the punishment.' As with the earlier oracles, the reminder is given that because of the multitude of sins, Ammon will not be spared divine judgment.[1] The first specific sin mentioned is what happened during territorial expansion ('that they might enlarge their border'). Genocide was practised, including the murder of pregnant women and their unborn babies. The Hebrew verb to denote this 'ripping open' (*bâqa'*) can be employed without any thought of violence against anyone (see its use for splitting wood, Gen. 22:3; ploughing, Psa. 141:7; chiselling out channels in rock, Job 28:10). However, it is used (in three of its themes, Qal, Pi'el, and Pu'al) for the barbarous practice of ripping open pregnant women (in addition to this passage, see 2 Kings 8:12; 15:16; Hos. 13:16 [Heb. 14:1]).

14. The standardised expression used in all the oracles against the nations in Amos is varied by the substitution in Hebrew of 'I will set [a fire]' for 'I will send.' It could point to the direct involvement of the LORD in the judgment instead of the use of secondary agents.[2] Rabbah

[1] For further information on the phrase, see the earlier comment on verses 3, 4.

[2] Another possible explanation is that at times deliberately altered standardised expressions were used. See the discussion by Stanislav Segert, 'A Controlling Device for Copying Stereotype Passages? (*Amos I 3-11-II 8, VI 1-6*),' *VT* 34 (1984), pp. 481-82.

was the capital. In David's time, the smaller states in the region were clearly engaged in a power struggle. At one time Ammon supported Israel (2 Sam. 10:2), but her king, Hanun, formed alliances with several Aramaean kingdoms. The long account of David's Ammonite war is given in 2 Samuel 8–12. It came to a successful conclusion when under Joab the royal citadel was captured (2 Sam. 12:26), followed by the full army under David who took the whole city (2 Sam. 12:29). That brought all of Ammon under David's control, which was denoted by him having the king of Ammon's golden crown placed on his head and the Ammonites forced to render forced labour (2 Sam. 12:30, 31). It remained part of the Davidic-Solomonic Empire, but later resumed independent status. Amos predicts the destruction of Rabbah, that probably took place by the Assyrians. The prophecy is that this will take place 'on the day of battle ... in the day of the whirlwind.' These are synonymous phrases, depicting the violent end that is to come. Much later in Old Testament history, the Ammonites feature in the prophecies of Jeremiah and Ezekiel (Jer. 49:2, 3; Ezek. 21:20; 25:1-7).

> 15. *'and their king shall go into exile, he and his princes together,' says the* L*ORD*.

The frequent consequence of defeat in battle in the Near East was that kings and people were taken into captivity, and often some of them were sold as slaves to other countries. In place of 'their king' (the people of Ammon) some of the ancient versions took this as a reference to the Ammonite god, who is called Molech in the Old Testament (1 Kings 11:7) or Milcom (1 Kings 11:5, 33). Such a reference to a divinity seems unlikely, as there are no depictions of gods being carried off into exile in any of the other oracles in Amos. The declarations concerning Ammon are rounded out with confirmation that this is indeed the word of the LORD.

f. Moab (2:1-3)

1, 2. *Thus says the LORD: 'For three transgressions of Moab, and for four, I will not revoke the punishment, because he burned to lime the bones of the king of Edom. So I will send a fire upon Moab, and it shall devour the strongholds of Kerioth, and Moab shall die amid uproar, amid shouting and the sound of the trumpet.'*

1. Like the Edomites, the Moabites were descendants of Abraham through the incestuous union of his nephew Lot with his daughters (see Gen. 19:30-38). Their territory was situated on a high plateau between the brooks Arnon and Zered, to the south-east of the Dead Sea. It was a relatively small piece of land, for even when it had expanded its territory, in size it was only approximately 3,600 sq. km. (1,400 sq. mi.). It was an irritant to Israel, requiring attention by both Saul (1 Sam. 14:47) and David (2 Sam. 8:2). Later, it rebelled against Israelite rule, and in the period after Elisha's death the Moabites were regularly making incursions into Israel (2 Kings 13:20). Not only here, but in other prophetic oracles of judgment, Moab is depicted as being the enemy of Israel (in addition to this passage, see Isa. 15–16; Zeph. 2:8-11; and Jer. 48).[1]

Moab's sin may seem at first sight to be somewhat trivial, in that 'he burned to lime the bones of the king of Edom.' What is described is an act of desecration of the bones of one of Edom's rulers. However, this was an act that showed no respect for the dead king, and Moab even wanted to use the lime produced in a building project. This is how the Targum interpreted the verse: 'because he burned the bones of the king of Edom and used them in the plaster of his house.' That is, the product of the fire was lime that

[1] For Isa. 15–16, see my remarks in *Isaiah: A Covenant to be Kept for the Sake of the Church* (Fearn: Christian Focus Publications, 2011), pp. 147-55; for Zeph. 2:8-11, O. Palmer Robertson, *The Books of Nahum, Habakkuk, and Zephaniah* (*NICOT*: Grand Rapids, 1990), pp. 301-09; and for Jer. 48, J. A. Thompson, *The Book of Jeremiah* (*NICOT*: Grand Rapids, Eerdmans, 1987), pp. 699-713.

was utilised in a building. No evidence exists to substantiate this, nor to try and pinpoint exactly when and where it happened. One important fact is that the condemnation of Moab was not for an offence against Israel, but for one against a non-Israelite community. God's concern for justice involved all the nations, not just his own special treasure.

2. The judgment is announced in the same terms as in 1:4, 7, 10, and 12: 'So I will send a fire upon Moab, and it shall devour the strongholds of Kerioth.' While more than one Kerioth is known (see Josh. 15:25, Kerioth Hezron), almost certainly this Kerioth was a village in Moab, as Jeremiah mentions it twice in his prophecy concerning Moab (Jer. 48:24, 41). It features in the Mesha inscription where the king of Moab writes of how he captured Ataroth in Israel and dragged an image of David to Kerioth.[1] The site has been identified as Qurêyat 'Alêyân, 11 km (7 miles) north-east of Dibon. It must have been a town of some size as it had fortresses, and these are predicted by Amos to fall to invaders. It is unclear if Kerioth was actually the capital of Moab. The cause of death is then traced explicitly to a battle with the reference to 'shouting and the sound of the trumpet.' In Israel the trumpet sound was used as a call to battle (Judg. 3:27; 1 Sam. 13:3; Jer. 42:14; 51:27), or as an alarm when enemies were approaching (Isa. 18:3; Jer. 4:5, 6; Ezek. 33:3-6; Hos. 5:8).

> 3. *'I will cut off the ruler from its midst, and will kill all its princes with him,' says the* Lord.

There is a sudden shift in person in this verse. In verse 1, a masculine singular form is used ('he burned'). Here, however, in verse 3 feminine singular forms occur ('her rulers,' 'her officials'). Such shifts

[1] The Mesha inscription commemorates the successful attempt by Mesha, King of Moab, to throw off the yoke of Israel. For this reference see J. C. L. Gibson, *Textbook of Syrian Semitic Inscriptions: Volume 1 Hebrew and Moabite Inscriptions* (Oxford: Clarendon Press, 1971), pp. 74-80, or *DOTT*, pp. 197-98.

are quite common in Hebrew poetry and prophecy. One plausible suggestion is that in verses 1, 2 the inhabitants are in view, and hence masculine forms occur. On the other hand, now the country is in view, and feminine singular forms are appropriate.[1] The judgment on people involves the rulers, called here by the title 'judge' (*shôfêt*). This seems to be a synonym for 'king,' as its usage in 2 Kings 15:5 and Daniel 9:12 suggests. Along with his officials, the king is to be killed. The first verb *kârat* means to cut someone off [from life], while the second verb is the common word for kill (*hârag*). Various attempts have been made to designate a particular historical event as being the fulfilment of this prophecy but no confirmation can be provided. Moab was certainly under Assyrian control while Tiglath-pileser III, Sennacherib, Esarhaddon, and Ashurbanipal were reigning.

Application

The last three oracles have been addressed to peoples related to Abraham—Edom, Ammon and Moab. Bringing condemnatory words against them was a reminder to Israel that kinship relationships do not determine standing with God. These three nations were not going to be spared God's judgment even though they could claim to be linked to God's people. This question of relationship arose in Jesus' day. John taught the Pharisees and Sadducees that simply making the claim, 'We have Abraham as our father,' would not ensure the raising up of godly offspring (Matt. 3:1-10). The same principle is expounded by the Apostle Paul, when he writes of the character of the true Jew: 'A man is not a Jew if he is only one outwardly, nor is circumcision merely outward and physical. No, a man is a Jew if he is one inwardly; and circumcision is circumcision of the heart, by the Spirit, not by the written

[1] This is the explanation given by Thomas J. Finley, *Joel, Amos, Obadiah*, p. 157. Countries are regarded as feminine in biblical Hebrew.

code. Such a man's praise is not from men, but from God' (Rom. 2:28, 29).

g. Judah (2:4, 5)

4, 5. *Thus says the* L*ORD*: *'For three transgressions of Judah, and for four, I will not revoke the punishment, because they have rejected the law of the* L*ORD*, *and have not kept his statutes, but their lies have led them astray, those after which their fathers walked. So I will send a fire upon Judah, and it shall devour the strongholds of Jerusalem.'*

Judgment comes closer and closer to Israel, but first it is directed against the southern kingdom of Judah. While both could claim their special relationship with God as a reason why they should be exempted from punishment, yet they too are condemned by their own actions.

4. The first part of the verse is identical with all the other oracles. Confirmation is given yet again that it is the LORD who speaks, and because of Judah's sins his wrath will not be turned back. The accusation follows. They have not kept God's law, nor have they obeyed the second commandment regarding the worship of other gods. Whereas the other nations already addressed had sinned against laws of humanity, Judah had sinned against divinely given laws. The verb 'reject' (Heb. *mâ'as*) is a strong expression. It is used of the rejection of the LORD in the days of Samuel (1 Sam 8:7; 10:19), and occurs again in Amos of God's despising Israel's feast days (Amos 5:21). In a context such as this, 'the law of the LORD' and 'his statutes' are synonymous (see the association of these terms in Deut. 17:19; Psa. 105:45). Judah spurned God's revelation, substituting her own ways for his.

One of the most blatant expressions of rebellion against divine law was turning to idolatry. Israel did it even when Moses was still on Mt. Sinai (Exod. 32:1-35), and on many later occasions. The message calls their idols 'their lies' (Heb. *kiz^{e}vêhem*), the only place in the Old Testament that does so. The fact that earlier generations are said to have 'walked after' idols shows clearly that idols are in view. 'To walk after' is Old Testament terminology for adhering to a particular god (see Deut. 8:19; 28:14; 1 Kings 11:10; 18:18; 21:26). Judah sinned, choosing an ethnic religion in preference to revealed religion.

5. The punishment is stated in the language that has already been used in the preceding six messages. Slight variations are evident, but the basic thrust is the same. Divinely initiated fire will be sent against Judah and the palaces of Jerusalem will be devoured.

h. Israel (2:6-16)

Up to this point, the people of Israel would have delighted in what Amos was saying about all the surrounding nations. The doom pronounced on others would have pleased them, but now Amos says that the same faults that brought God's judgment on their neighbours are exhibited by them. Israel, the chosen nation (3:2), was no better, and would inevitably suffer too for her sins. Because the prophet is coming to the climactic point of his message, the sins of Israel and Judah are spelt out in far greater detail than those of the other nations. The opening verses of the message give four reasons for the indictment.

> 6. *Thus says the* Lord*: 'For three transgressions of Israel, and for four, I will not revoke the punishment, because they sell the righteous for silver, and the needy for a pair of sandals.'*

The first reason is the perverse practice of selling others into slavery. While Israelites could sell their own services and work, this arrangement was cancelled in its seventh year (Deut. 15:12). Voluntary servitude was not to be for an indefinite time. However, what

Amos appears to have in view is the selling of others: 'they sell the righteous for silver, and the needy for a pair of sandals.' It is uncertain just how the parallel expressions, righteous/needy and silver/ pair of sandals, are to be interpreted. As the relationship with God is not the primary focus, 'righteous' is most probably a description of an innocent person, whose debt had been incurred because payment had been extorted from them by creditors. The expression 'needy' refers to a state of need, to those who have fallen on hard times (see Job 30:15). The reference to 'a pair of sandals' is perplexing. Attention has been drawn to Ruth 4:7, the description of a symbolic exchange of a sandal as a seal in the transfer of property, but only one sandal was involved in that procedure. No property transaction is in view here (see comments on 8:6). 'A pair of sandals' seems rather just to point to something of insignificant value, a debt that a creditor should have been prepared to write off. For a trifling sum, such a poor person was given into slavery.[1]

> 7. *'those who trample the head of the poor into the dust of the earth and turn aside the way of the afflicted; a man and his father go in to the same girl, so that my holy name is profaned.'*

The second reason relates to another form of oppression of the poor, or else it is a generalisation expounding the previous verse. The accusation is that people are crushing the poor against the dust of the earth. Various suggestions have been made about the first verb (Heb. *hashsho'afîm*), with emendations being proposed.[2] However, the verb 'crush' (Heb. *shâ'af*) is well attested in Biblical Hebrew (Psa. 56:2, 3; 57:4; Ezek. 36:3). 'The head of the poor' are said to be crushed 'into the dust of the earth.' This is hyperbole, an

[1] For fuller discussion of the various possible interpretations of this verse, see Thomas J. Finley, *Joel, Amos, Obadiah*, pp. 162-65.

[2] See *BHS*[5], which relates it to the root *shûf* I, 'to crush.' For a similar interpretation, see Douglas Stuart, *Hosea-Jonah* (WBC: Waco: Word Books, 1987), p. 307.

obvious exaggeration to make the point that, instead of protecting the weak, the rich and powerful trample over them. A similar accusation is made by Amos' fellow 8th-century prophet, Isaiah, as he rebuked the people of Jerusalem: '"What do you mean by crushing my people by grinding the face of the poor?" declares the Lord GOD of hosts' (Isa. 3:15). In both Israel and Judah, those with power utilised their positions, achieving their own aggrandisement by oppressing the poor. The parallel phrase, 'turn aside the way of the afflicted,' reinforces the point. Literally the translation is, 'and the way of the oppressed they turn aside.' Though the parallel expressions for those being treated unjustly are 'poor'/'oppressed,' the combination of another word for 'poor' (*'evyôn*) and 'oppressed' (*'ᵒnî*) occurs often as a standardised expression (see Deut. 15:11; Job 24:4; Psa. 12:5; Isa. 41:17; Ezek. 16:49). The 'way' of the oppressed in this context refers to the manner in which the oppressed tried to seek justice. Any attempt by them to achieve a just resolution of a difficulty was diverted (see the same use of this verb 'turn aside,' Heb. *nâtâh*, hi., in Isa. 10:2). The sins of Israel went much further, for a man and his son could be involved with the same temple prostitute. This practice was a Canaanite one, but Israel was not immune to such gross sensuality. The biblical text itself tells little about the practice, though cult prostitution was forbidden (Deut. 23:17).[1] King Asa expelled male prostitutes from the land (1 Kings 15:12), while his son Jehoshaphat got rid of those that remained (1 Kings 22:46). In Amos' day this type of fertility cult was practised, and it was a dishonour to the LORD and his name.

[1] The Heb. word for a male cult prostitute was *qâdêsh* and the feminine *qᵉdêshâh*. Both words are derived from the Heb. word *qâdôsh*, 'holy.' Though serving at the holy place, and thus named in reference to it, these men and women were anything but holy, and true Israelites should have avoided participating in this blatant public act of immorality.

8. *'they lay themselves down beside every altar on garments taken in pledge, and in the house of their God they drink the wine of those who have been fined.'*

This sexual activity was taking place on garments taken in pledge. The law relating to things pledged was given in Exodus 22:25, 26 and Deuteronomy 24:12, 13. The general principle was that a person borrowing by giving some possessions as security still had rights that had to be observed. In the case in point here, garments taken in pledge could not be kept overnight (see also Job 22:6). In an extra-biblical document found south of Tel Aviv, a complaint is made to the governor that an official retained the garment of a farm worker overnight. The sin in Israel went further, in that such garments were the bed on which they lay. The use of the same verb (*nâtâh*, hi.) in successive verses draws attention to perversion of justice and God's law.[1] Moreover, the holy place of worship was being further defiled by becoming a place of drunken revelry. Drink taken as a fine, or bought with money paid for a fine, was being consumed at the altar. There is a parallelism between the phrases dealing with the sexual sins and the drunken debauchery. Abuse of strong drink and sexual immorality were closely connected. Though still coming to the altar that was devoted to the LORD, the people in Amos' time were in effect imitating the behaviour of those who were devoted to Baal.

9. *'Yet it was I who destroyed the Amorite before them, whose height was like the height of the cedars and who was as strong as the oaks; I destroyed his fruit above and his roots beneath.'*

Verses 9-12 contain as a contrast a rehearsal of God's gracious dealings on behalf of his people. This serves to highlight the gross ingratitude of the people, namely their folly in turning aside from

[1] This is hard to bring out in English translation. Those who 'turn aside the way of the humble' (NASB, verse 7) are also the ones who 'turn aside' to lie down on garments taken in pledge.

their Saviour. Verses 9 and 10 both start with a Hebrew expression (*vᵉ'ânokî*) in which the separate pronoun 'I', preceded by the conjunction *vᵉ* ('and' or 'but'), draws attention to the LORD's saving and redeeming work. In contrast to what the people have been doing in flouting his laws, it was he who had shown such compassion to them. Mighty enemies were destroyed as Israel came into the land of Canaan, among them the Amorites. The conquest of the Amorites is recounted in Numbers 21:23-26 and in Deuteronomy 2:24-37. They are described here in poetic language which depicts their strength ('was like the height of the cedars and who was as strong as the oaks'). The reference to destruction of the fruit and the roots implies that the present power of the Amorites in Amos' day was curtailed by the LORD ('his fruit'), while the future would be limited because of the destruction of 'his roots.'

> 10. *'Also it was I who brought you up out of the land of Egypt and led you for forty years in the wilderness, to possess the land of the Amorite.'*

The LORD reminds Israel of his great redemptive activity in saving them out of the slavery and bondage that they endured in Egypt. This became a standard way of describing what actually happened at the time of the exodus. It was part of the promise to enslaved Israel (Exod. 3:8), and became enshrined as the opening of the Decalogue (Exod. 20:2; Deut. 5:6). Not only that, but the LORD led them for forty years in the wilderness, and gave them a land in which to live, including the land of the Amorites. This was all part of God's gracious provision for his people and evidence of the sovereign love he had bestowed on them (Deut. 7:9).

> 11. *'And I raised up some of your sons for prophets, and some of your young men for Nazirites. Is it not indeed so, O people of Israel?' declares the LORD.*

Two special acts of God's providential dealing with Israel are cited. The first was the provision of a prophetic ministry. This was established as a means of revelation, in direct contrast to the heathen practices of the Canaanites (see Deut. 18:9-18). God's word was to be given to the prophet, who then would declare it to the people. The work of the prophet was clearly portrayed in the way in which Aaron acted as Moses' prophet (Exod. 4:14-17). The second provision was for Nazirites, the law regarding them being given in Numbers 6:1-21.[1] These were people, male or female, who dedicated themselves to the LORD, and refrained from acts such as drinking alcohol or cutting their hair. Little information is given in the Old Testament of how often the law of Numbers 6 was actually acted upon, nor is there any indication by Amos of how many people had dedicated themselves in his time to be Nazirites. The only specific fact he gives is that they were 'young men.' The final words of this verse are a question: '"Is it not indeed so, O people of Israel?" declares the LORD.' The people in Amos' day are called upon to confirm these facts, and to acknowledge that God's graciousness had indeed been manifest in them. The concluding phrase, 'declares the LORD,' utilises the word *n^e'um* that is used by the prophets accompanying a message of divine origin and authority. While it occurs 314 times in the Old Testament, all but twenty of these occurrences are in the prophecies of Isaiah (23 times), Amos (21 times), Jeremiah (167 times), Ezekiel (83 times), and Zechariah (20 times). The word *n^e'um* is a noun, not a verb, and should strictly be translated 'an utterance,' 'a [divine] word.'

12. *'But you made the Nazirites drink wine, and commanded the prophets saying, "You shall not prophesy."'*

[1] For discussion of this chapter, see in particular John Currid, *Numbers* (Darlington: EP Study Commentary, 2009), pp. 101-08), and R. K. Harrison, *Numbers,* The Wycliffe Exegetical Commentary: Chicago: Moody Press, 1990), pp. 121-31, and his 'Excursus on the Nazirite Law,' pp. 134-35.

The two blessings given to Israel that have just been mentioned were despised by the people. Though they knew the law governing the Nazirites, they went out of their way to make them drink wine. Those appointed to exemplify a godly life were deliberately debauched. Likewise, with the prophets, the very spokesmen appointed to declare God's word were silenced. The form of the command is interesting, because instead of the normal grammatical one (Heb. *'al* + juss.), it is modelled on the divine commands such as in the Decalogue (*lo'* + imperf.). They were saying to the prophets: 'You must not prophesy at all!'[1]

13. *'Behold, I will press you down in your place, as a cart full of sheaves presses down.'*

The threat of divine judgment is given in two ways. In this verse the people are going to be crushed by direct action of God, while in verses 14-16 military intervention is going to achieve God's purposes. The first of these announcements carries emphasis: 'Behold, I ...' The introductory exclamation (Heb. *hinnêh*) is a word to arrest attention before a declaration, especially a divine one. While 'behold' has been the common rendering, it is now an antiquated form, and something more colloquial is required. 'Look now,' or 'Now then' (NIV), are nearer the mark. The form for 'I' is an emphatic one (*'ânokî*, not *'ᵃnî*).[2] This is picking up on the same emphasis at the beginning of verses 9 and 10. The words that follow have given difficulty to translators since the early Christian centuries, as comparison of versions shows. The difficulties are threefold: the first is that the Hebrew verb translated as 'press you down' (Heb. *'ûq*), in the ESV only occurs here in the Old Testament; secondly, it is uncertain as

[1] The translation is that of J. Niehaus in T. E. McComiskey, ed., 'Amos,' *An Exegetical and Expository Commentary: The Minor Prophets* (Grand Rapids: Baker, 1992), pp. 370-71.

[2] If no emphasis was needed, the normal way of expressing 'Behold, I ...' would be *hinenî*, as in Isa. 6:8.

to the particular meaning of the preposition *tachat* plus suffix, that is rendered simply by 'you' in the ESV translation; and, thirdly, it is unclear in the second colon what the cart crushes. While questions of Hebrew philology are involved in any interpretation, the context must also be a guide, as the picture is clearly of an overloaded wagon that serves to illustrate the nature of God's judgment.

While numerous suggestions have been made concerning this verse, and, in particular, the meaning of the verb 'press down' (Heb. *'ûq*), none have proved any more satisfactory than the traditional rendering.[1] The appearance of two nouns seemingly from the same root in the Psalms tends to support this position (*'âqâh* in Psa. 55:4, and *mû'âqâh* in Psa. 66:11). However, the rendering of the AV, 'Behold, I am pressured under you,' followed by the RV, NASB and NKJV cannot be accepted, as the form of the verb is a causative participle (Heb. *mê'îq*, hi.), not a passive. It is a declaration by God of what he intended to do. The ESV translation gives a satisfactory meaning to both the verb ('press down') and the prepositional phrase ('your place'), as well as fitting in admirably in the context. The use of an imagery from rural life is typical in Amos (see 3:8, 12; 5:19), while the concept is that divinely ordained pressure will prevent the people in any way providing for their own protection.[2] In whatever way the impending judgment comes, the people will be powerless to resist it.

14. *'Flight shall perish from the swift, and the strong shall not retain his strength, nor shall the mighty save his life.'*

[1] For the possible translations, see *DCH*, VI, p. 314. For an older listing of the possibilities, see W. R. Harper, *A Critical and Exegetical Commentary on Amos and Hosea* (Edinbugh: T. & T. Clark, 1973 reprint), pp. 60-61, and R. S. Cripps, *A Critical and Exegetical Commentary on the Book of Amos: The Text of the Revised Version edited with Introduction, Notes, and Excurses*, 2nd ed. (London: SPCK, 1969 reprint), pp. 147-48; and for more recent ones, E. Hammershaimb, *The Book of Amos: A Commentary* (Oxford: Blackwells, 1970), pp. 54-55.

[2] This is the interpretation that J. Niehaus, 'Amos,' p. 371, advances.

Now the picture becomes explicitly one of military intervention in the history of Israel, and it is clearly a continuation from what has just been announced in verse 13. The form of expression, 'and the swift' (Heb. *v^eqal*), links this verse with what has just preceded it. The general idea is that a disaster is impending from which none shall escape. No matter how fleet of foot anyone is, they will be unable to evade capture, while the strong will find that they cannot summon up any renewed strength to help in battle. Even the mighty warriors will fail in the attempt to save their own lives. This could be because of fright, or because of realisation that the enemy force was overwhelmingly strong. Literally, the Hebrew text has, 'and the mighty man will not save his soul.' The Hebrew word '*nefesh*' is not the human spirit, as the English noun may suggest, but rather his being—his life. Self-preservation will be beyond the experienced warrior (Heb. *gibbôr*; see the use of this noun in Gen. 6:4; 10:8; Isa. 9:5).

> 15. *'he who handles the bow shall not stand, and he who is swift of foot shall not save himself, nor shall he who rides the horse save his life.'*

Again, the continuity in the narrative is marked by the opening phrase, 'he who handles the bow' (Heb. *v^etofês haqqeshet*). Further descriptions are to be given of the inability of any person in Israel to escape from the coming judgment. The verb 'handle' (Heb. *tâfas*) is used in a wide variety of passages to indicate holding a weapon of war (Ezek. 21:15; 38:4). Archers were very prominent in the armies of Israel, Judah, and the surrounding nations, as both documents and drawings attest. Even though armed for battle, those who carry the bow will not be able to hold their ground (Heb. lit. 'stand,' *'âmad*) when attacks come. Likewise, the 'swift of foot,' the soldier, will not be able to escape by running from the battlefield.[1] Nor will

[1] The Heb. text has simply 'the fleet-footed,' but it is clearly correct to understand this as a reference to the soldiers (see NIV, 'fleet-footed soldiers'). The expression

the cavalryman have the capacity to escape either. While horses and chariots were not used as extensively in Israel and Judah (partly because of cost, and partly because of the geography), it is clear that they were used to some extent.

16. *'and he who is stout of heart among the mighty shall flee away naked in that day,' declares the* L*ORD*.

The final description of representatives in Israel is of 'the stout of heart.' Again, the context suggests 'brave warriors' (NIV), though the Hebrew text simply has 'the stout [in respect to] his heart among the mighty (*baggibbôrîm*).' This is in reality a superlative expression, 'the bravest among the mighty ones.' The brave warriors will flee for their lives, leaving their tunics behind. This, rather than the ideas of nakedness, is meant by the expression 'shall flee away naked.' To get away from an enemy it might be necessary to get rid of one's outer garment. The time this will happen is expressed as 'in that day' (*bayyôm hahû'*), which is probably not the great, final Day of the LORD, but the day when the Assyrians come and wreak vengeance on Israel. The proclamation of these threats is rounded off with the formula, 'declares the LORD' (for comment see the end of verse 11).

Application

This passage is the first in this book that is directed to God's own people. Even though the division of the kingdom on Solomon's death was tragic, and much of the blame for it lay with the northern tribes, yet God did not cast off his people. Like many other Old Testament passages, God reminds the people of all the past blessings they have

'shall not save' (*lo' ye mallêt*) is the same as in the previous verse, but lacks the addition of *nafshô*, 'his life.' The fact that it occurs in the first and third occurrences of this idiom here in verses 14, 15 suggests that it is a double-duty expression that was meant to be taken for granted here in verse 15.

received from him—exodus from Egypt, providential care in the wilderness, entry into the land of Canaan, the gift of prophets. How grateful they should have been! But instead they rejected his authority and despised his laws. Privileges received do not guarantee future blessings. Israel in Amos' day needed a sharp reality check. Though they must have been surprised by the message, the certainty of judgment was proclaimed. So must we recall the Scripture that says: 'For it is time for judgment to begin at the household of God; and if it begins with us, what will be the outcome for those who do not obey the gospel of God?' (1 Pet. 4:17). We live our lives *coram Deo*, 'in the presence of God.'

3

Oracles Against the Chosen People (3:1–5:17)

1. *Breach of the Covenant (3:1-15)*

a. God's Punishment Announced (3:1, 2)

A new part of the prophecy commences at this point, and extends through to 5:17. Three sections are marked out by the introductory formula, 'Hear this word' (*shimeʿû et haddâvâr hazzeh*) in 3:1, 4:1, and 5:1. It also contains two 'woe' passages (5:18-27 and 6:1-14).

The opening verses of chapter 3 are closely connected to other similar passages in the Old Testament, in which a court-room scene is depicted. The LORD has a controversy with his people and calls on witnesses to confirm the breaches of covenantal regulations that have taken place. While using the same Hebrew word for 'covenant' (*beʳrît*), various relationships can be included—nation with nation, individual with individual, and God with his people. These covenants were widely known and utilised in the Ancient Near East, and so a familiar device was introduced into the theological language. This resulted in quicker and more accurate appreciation by the people of the covenantal bond they had with the LORD. He was accommodating himself to their weakness by introducing a common relationship framework that was unusually appropriate for divine-human bonds.

1. *Hear this word that the* Lord *has spoken against you, O people of Israel, against the whole family that I brought up out of the land of Egypt.*

The opening imperative, 'Hear,' is used here as it is in other covenantal lawsuit passages (e.g. Isa. 1:2; Mic. 6:2) to arrest attention to the message that the Lord had spoken. This word was directed to the people of Israel. The preposition used (*'al*) can mean 'to,' but it can also mean 'against,' and this is the preferable interpretation here.[1] The further explanation of who constituted 'Israel' was that it was 'the whole family that I brought up out of the land of Egypt' (lit. 'all the families'). The switch from third-person ('the Lord spoke') to first-person ('I brought up') may seem sudden but it is not without parallel. After announcing that God had spoken, Amos now voices words that are presented as God's own declaration. The message is directed to a redeemed people. Israel had been 'brought up out of Egypt,' one of the common phrases used in the Old Testament to describe the exit of Israel from Egypt (see the use of this expression already in 2:10).

2. *'You only have I known of all the families of the earth; therefore I will punish you for all your iniquities.'*

The first point Israel needed to hear again was the exclusive nature of her relationship with the Lord: 'You only …' The word 'only' is a particle in Hebrew (*raq*) that often precedes a noun, or, as in this case, a phrase that forms the object of the verb. Since it commences the sentence, the emphasis in English translation should be placed on it: '*Only* you …' The verb that follows, 'known' (*yâda'*), in addition to its general use, also has a very specific connotation. It is employed to indicate God's close knowledge of, and relationship with, his chosen people. That is why versions such as the NIV use the translation

[1] For all the varied meanings of this preposition, including that in this verse, see *DCH*, VI, pp. 385-98.

'chose.' Israel was chosen, not because of her superior size to other nations, but simply because God set his love upon her (Deut. 7:7).[1] Hence, before enlarging on the accusations that have already been made against Israel (2:12-16), a reminder is given to the people of the exclusive relationship between themselves and the LORD. The fact that those addressed—you (pl.)—were not the original recipients of the covenantal revelation is consistent with Old Testament teaching. Succeeding generations were just as much related to the LORD by covenant as the original one was (see Deut. 5:2, 3).

The second part of the verse would have been a complete surprise to most of Amos' hearers. For them the consequence of Israel's election by God would be abundant blessing. What they failed to understand was that election to privilege also brought with it election to responsibility. Now they are confronted by the prospect of divine visitation in judgment: 'Therefore I will punish you ...' God's covenants were not unconditional, but rested on reciprocal adherence to the covenantal requirements.[2] Because of Israel's failure to fulfil the terms, punishment was in store. The ESV 'punish' represents the Hebrew *pâqad*, a verb that occurs over three hundred times in the Old Testament, but yet it is not an easy word to translate.[3] Here the idiom is 'to visit upon' (*pâqad 'al*) in the sense of 'inflict punishment on.'[4] Such punishment is said to

[1] For discussion of 'know' as a covenantal term, see H. Huffmon, 'The treaty background of Hebrew *yâda'*,' *BASOR* 181 (1966), pp. 31-37.

[2] See the article by Richard Pratt, 'Were the covenants with Abraham and David conditional?' Benyamin F. Intan, ed., *God's Fiery Challenger: Festschrift in honor of Stephen Tong* (Jakarta: Reformed Center for Religion and Society, 2007), pp. 139-67.

[3] E. A. Speiser considered that there 'is no other Hebrew verb that has caused translators so much trouble as *pqd*' ('Census and Ritual Expiation in Mari and Israel,' *BASOR* 149 (1958), p. 21). See also, the entry in *DCH*, VI, pp. 737-45 and the full bibliography on pp. 938-39.

[4] For discussion of the idiom, see T. E. McComiskey, 'Prophetic Irony in Hosea 1:4: A Study of the Collocation *pâqad 'al* and its Implications for the Fall of Jehu's Dynasty,' *JETS* 58 (1993), pp. 93-110.

be in response to 'your sins' (*ʿ*[a]*vônᵉtêkem*). This is one of a cluster of terms that can be used for sin and transgression (see the group of nouns used in Psa. 51:2, 3), and its basic meaning is 'crooked behaviour,' or 'perversion.'

b. Penetrating Questions (3:3-6)

A series of rhetorical questions presses the point home. Nothing in life is haphazard, and Amos' illustrations are drawn from things with which he and his audience were very familiar. If *this* happens, then *that* is the consequence. Sins of intemperance, immorality, and oppression of the poor will incur God's judgment. The questions asked of the people all demand a negative response.

3. *'Do two walk together, unless they have agreed to meet?'*

The first illustration concerns two men who walk together because they have made a pact to do so. They have an appointment. The verb (*yâʿad*, ni.) is used of meeting God at the sanctuary (Exod. 25:22; 29:43). God met with his people there, for he always kept his appointments. The LXX had a different rendering of this clause: 'Will two walk together unless they *know* one another?' This means that the LXX translators were taking the verb as from the root *y-d-ʿ*, not from *y-ʿ-d*, simply transposing the consonants. While it makes good sense in the context, the Hebrew manuscript evidence does not confirm this.

4. *'Does a lion roar in the forest, when he has no prey? Does a young lion cry out from his den, if he has taken nothing?'*

While the lion has long been extinct in Israel, yet Amos and his hearers must have been familiar with it. The illustrations look like ones that Amos, the shepherd, could have experienced himself. He asks whether the adult lion (*'aryêh*) roars in the thicket (or brush) without having caught anything, such as some juicy prey. Likewise, does the young lion (*kᵉfîr*) growl in its den if it hasn't caught anything? Of course not! Amos is establishing the principle that every event has a cause. Some commentators have wanted to make the lion the LORD, with the prey being Israel, but even though the LORD is compared with a lion who roars (1:2), no such connection is even hinted at in this verse.

> 5. *'Does a bird fall in a snare on the earth, when there is no trap for it? Does a snare spring up from the ground, when it has taken nothing?'*

The imagery changes to bird life. Two kinds of traps are in view. The first one is a mechanism whereby a bird touching part of the trap allows it to fall and it is captured. The second one is probably the type of net that is known to have been used extensively in Egypt, though some think that it was a stick that flew up and killed the bird. In both cases, the same point is being made as in the previous verse. Events are precipitated by prior actions.

> 6. *'Is a trumpet blown in a city, and the people are not afraid? Does disaster come to a city, unless the Lord has done it?'*

Another illustration is drawn from what happened when an attack by an enemy army was imminent. The *shôphâr*, the ram's horn, was used to give signals in both civic and military affairs. It was used to announce the new month and the new year, but it was also used to alert the people to some impending disaster. Amos is stating an obvious fact. A danger signal causes trepidation among the population. The second colon declares that disaster, when it comes, is under God's sovereign control. The AV renders it: 'Shall there be evil in a city.' The word for 'evil' (*ra'*), while often meaning 'bad,' also has the connotation of a tragic event, or some disastrous occurrence. In Isaiah 45:7 the LORD is the one who brings 'peace' (*shâlôm*) and 'disaster' (*ra'*), and so here in Amos 3:6 (see also Job

2:10). The usual translation of 'city' (Heb. *'îr*) is too grandiose a word. The meaning is much closer to our word 'town.' These statements contain a dreadful warning if only the people could grasp it. Disaster was indeed coming on Israel because of rebellion and sin, and it would be the LORD's doing.

c. The Disclosure of God's Will (3:7, 8)

Just as nothing happens in nature without some forewarning, so with the revelation of God's purposes for his people. He does not leave his people in darkness concerning his purposes, but uses the means of communication he has appointed to reveal his will.

> 7. *'For the Lord GOD does nothing without revealing his secret to his servants the prophets. The lion has roared; who will not fear? The Lord God has spoken; who can but prophesy?'*

The message concerning judgment for Israel that Amos has been hinting at comes to a climax in these verses. He makes it clear that the Lord GOD uses his appointed spokesmen, the prophets, to announce his intended purposes. 'Lord GOD' is the way in which the ESV and many other versions translate the combination in Hebrew of the word for 'Lord' (*'ᵃdonây*) and the divine name, *yhwh*. Usually the latter alone is rendered 'LORD,' but this has to change when *'ᵃdonây* is used along with *yhwh*. What Amos was asserting was that God uncovered or revealed (*gâlâh*) his secret counsel (*sôd*) to 'his servants the prophets' (*'el 'ᵃvâdâv hannᵉvî'îm*). This is a very important statement of how God acted, and through whom he ministered his word. The institution of prophecy was God's appointed way of declaring his will (Deut. 18:15-22). Amos has just told his audience that disasters were caused by the LORD, and now he adds that forewarning of such events is given by prophetic disclosure. That being so, how eagerly the people should have listened to Amos' message!

In verse 8 Amos presses the point in regard to the compulsion he was under to make God's message known. In an echo of 1:2, he speaks of the fear that a roaring lion creates. When that lion is the Lord GOD, what could his servant Amos do but prophesy? When God had spoken the prophet could not remain silent. Later, Amos will develop God's message further. At this point in his prophecy, the message is that the people should recognise that God has spoken a message of judgment, and they should respond with fear and repentance.

Application

Two important points come out of this passage. The first is that a privileged position in God's sight brings great responsibility. Israel of old often forgot this basic truth, and acted in a manner more like their heathen neighbours. They were to carry God's name by their obedience to his revealed will (Exod. 20:7; Deut. 5:11). No less is the principle carried over into the New Testament. While believers may be saints in God's sight, yet their lives must display the change in character that has come through the new birth, not the actions that characterised them formerly (see Eph. 2:1-3). Temptations may come, and even when believers think they are standing firm, they have to be careful lest they fall (1 Cor. 10:12).

The second truth is that God, who spoke by his servants the prophets, has spoken finally in his own Son, the Lord Jesus (Heb. 1:1, 2). No need exists for another word of prophecy for Christians because the revelation of the Lord Jesus we have in the Scripture is final, and nothing is to be added to it or subtracted from it (Rev. 22:18, 19). Gospel proclamation today should be a declaration of what God has given in the Bible, for the things written are that we may 'believe that Jesus is the

Christ, the Son of God, and that by believing you may have life in his name' (John 20:31).

d. Just Punishment (3:9-15)

In semi-legal language Amos challenges Israel and warns of her impending judgment in the form of an invading army. Only a few will escape the plundering troops. Past visitations of God had not really changed the heart of the people, and sins previously committed and condemned were being practised again.

9. *Proclaim to the strongholds in Ashdod and to the strongholds in the land of Egypt, and say, 'Assemble yourselves on the mountains of Samaria, and see the great tumults within her, and the oppressed in her midst.'*

In covenantal legal proceedings it was common to appeal to witnesses, sometimes inanimate ones like the heavens and the earth (see Deut. 32:1; Isa. 1:2). Here Amos appeals to silent witnesses in the Philistine city of Ashdod[1] and Egypt, imagining them assembling on the hills of Samaria[2] to see 'the great tumults' that the LORD was bringing, as well as the 'oppressed' within her. Samaria was in a geographical central position for both the administration of the country and for international contacts. The word 'tumults' (*m*ᵉ*hûmâh*) comes from a verb that conveys the idea of creating a great disturbance. The noun occurs twelve times, and in ten of them it is used of God's actions against his enemies (see Deut. 7:23), or against Israel (Deut. 28:20).

[1] Instead of 'in Ashdod,' the LXX has 'in Assyria' (*en assuriois*). While this only involves the change of one consonant in Hebrew (altering *b*ᵉ*'ashdôd* to *b*ᵉ*'ashshûr*), no other manuscript can be cited to support it. Ashdod may have been chosen because of its similarity to the Hebrew word for violence (*shod*) in verse 10. This was pointed out by G. A. Smith, *The Book of the Twelve Prophets*, vol. 1 (New York: A. C. Armstrong and Son, 1896), p. 145.

[2] Again, the LXX differs from the MT in that it has 'the *hill* of Samaria,' rather than the plural, 'the *hills* of Samaria.' This was probably an attempt at harmonisation, as 4:1 and 6:1 both have the singular, 'the *hill* of.'

The force of the plural imperative, 'See,' carries into the next clause: '[See] the oppressed in her midst.' No indication is given in the text who the perpetrator of the oppression is, but the context suggests that it is people within Israel who are acting in such a heartless and cruel fashion (see the use again in 4:1 of the same idea).

10. *'They do not know how to do right,' declares the* Lord, *'those who store up violence and robbery in their strongholds.'*

The Lord's declaration concerning Samaria was that the people 'do not know how to do right.' They refused to follow the straight (*n^ekochâh*) path, choosing rather to deviate from the prescribed way. What they have taken forcibly from others, they store up in their fortresses. In addition to the play on the place name Ashdod with the use of 'violence' (*shod*), further paronomasia occurs in the use of 'the stored things' (*hâ'ôtsrîm*) that echoes the word 'Egypt' (*mitsrayîm*).

11. *Therefore thus says the Lord* God: *'An adversary shall surround the land and bring down your defences from you, and your strongholds shall be plundered.'*

The lion who roared (verse 4) brings a message of judgment and devastation for the northern kingdom. This is introduced by the particle 'therefore' (*lâkên*), that is frequently used in the Old Testament prophetical books to introduce a divine declaration (see Isa. 5:13, 14, 24; 7:14; 10:16; Jer. 7:32), often marking the transition from discussion to the punitive announcement. The Lord God (for the explanation of this form of address, see verse 8) knew the unscrupulous practices of the nobles, and their love of wealth and pleasure. The first part of the message is awkward: 'An adversary—and a surrounding of the land!' 'Adversary' (*tsar*) could be translated as the noun 'distress,' as the forms are identical in Hebrew. However, in view of the context, it is best to think of a personal enemy rather than the abstract idea of distress. The following phrase has evoked various emendations, one in particular following the Syriac (Peshitta) translation, 'will surround.'[1] Probably the best way to understand it is as a cry of alarm, as if someone was alerting everyone of the impending disaster.[2] The phrase, 'and a surrounding of the land,' or 'even a surrounding of the land,' would alert the people to the fact that the invasion was not just going to be localised in the region of Samaria but would extend to the whole land. The rest of the message is plain enough and is directly addressed to Israel ('*your* strongholds,' '*your* fortresses'; Heb. second pers. sing. suffixes). No defences will be able to stand up to the invader, and mighty buildings that seemed impregnable will fall. It is almost as if Amos was delivering a message with the sound of the troops ringing in his ears, as he heard them smashing their way into every corner of the land. The covenantal curse of Deuteronomy 28:52 will come to fulfilment: 'They shall besiege you in all your towns, until your high and fortified walls, in which you trusted, come down throughout all your land. And they shall besiege you in all your towns throughout all your land, which the LORD your God has given you.'

> 12. *Thus says the LORD: 'As the shepherd rescues from the mouth of the lion two legs, or a piece of an ear, so shall the people of Israel who dwell in Samaria be rescued, with the corner of a couch and part of a bed.'*

The LORD's declaration concerning Israel is that the result of the invasion will be like a shepherd rescuing only small parts of animals killed by a lion—'two legs or a piece of an ear.' The analogy does not need to be taken to the extreme of suggesting that no one would be

[1] This involves altering the MT from *ûs^evîv hâ'ârets* to *y^esôvêv hâ'ârets*. The evidence is not strong, as no Hebrew manuscripts have this reading. Both the NIV and the ESV, however, accept the emendation.

[2] This is the position taken by T. J. Finley, *Joel, Amos, Obadiah*, p. 190.

rescued after the invasion. More probably the use of small parts of the animals just indicates that any remnant of Israel will be small and insignificant. The verb for 'deliver' (Heb. *nâtsal*, hi.) recalls God's redemption of his people from Egypt, being very close in meaning to two of the verbs for 'redeem' (*gâ'al* and *pâdâh*). Perhaps the common response to a message like this was, 'God *will* save us.' However, now the message that comes through Amos is that there will indeed be salvation, but a quite different one from that of popular expectation. 'As (*ka'ᵃsher*) the shepherd rescues ... so (*kên*) shall the people of Israel who dwell in Samaria be rescued.' The only remnant of Israel will be like the mutilated parts of animals that have been mauled by lions.

The final part of verse 12 is difficult, as the ESV footnote acknowledges: 'The meaning of the Hebrew for this word is uncertain.' The major difficulty is the Hebrew word *dᵉmesheq*. It sounds like the word *Damascus*, but in Hebrew this is usually *dammeseq* (with the consonant *sin*, not *shin*, and with a doubled *m*).[1] Several factors count against regarding this as the place name Damascus. First of all, the word 'Damascus' has already occurred in 1:3, and it would be very unusual to now spell it differently. Secondly, parallelism exists in the latter part of this verse, and it suggests a word such as 'corner' is what is needed in the context.

> *'those who sit in Samaria*
> *on the edge of their beds*
> *and in ... couch.'*

What is required is a word that matches in some way 'the edge of,' and this was suggested by the medieval Jewish scholar Ibn Ezra.[2]

[1] The matter is complicated further by two variant spellings of Damascus in the MT. In 1 Chron. 18:5 the name is given as *darmesheq*, while in 2 Kings 16:10 the form is *dûrmesheq*.

[2] This was noted by the English scholar, E. B. Pusey, *The Minor Prophets: A Commentary* (Grand Rapids: Baker Book House, 1950 reprint), p. 277.

Thirdly, the order of words is correct if the AV translation is followed, 'in the corner of a bed, and *in* Damascus in a couch,' though the preposition 'in' has to be understood in the second phrase. However, it has been suggested that the translation be, 'in a Damascus couch,' but this requires the words 'Damascus' and 'couch' to be reversed in the Hebrew text.

Of all the possibilities, it is best to assume that a translation is needed that forms a parallel with 'the edge of,' and hence 'the corner of' is a good fit. This explanation recognises that the word here is a *hapax legomenon* in the Old Testament, and in the absence of any other occurrence the general meaning has to be the major guide.[1] The picture is of people indulging in a lavish lifestyle, reclining on their couches, and totally unaware that sudden judgment is coming. Later Amos returns to the theme of expensive living when he condemns the complacency of those in Zion (6:1-7).

13. *'Hear, and testify against the house of Jacob,' declares the Lord GOD, the God of hosts.*

The threat against Israel calls forth another declaration by the LORD. The nation was reminded of its covenantal heritage by the use of the phrase 'the house of Jacob,' and perhaps it was intended to be inclusive of all the tribes, thus implicitly referring to Judah as well as to Israel. Whereas up to 2:6 the announcements were all mainly in the same form ('Thus says the LORD'), now greater variety in the designations for God occur. A full one appears here: 'Lord GOD, God of hosts' (*'ᵃdônay yhwh 'ᵉlôhê hatstsᵉvâ'ôt*). The phrase 'God of hosts' occurs 18 times in the Old Testament, placing emphasis on his

[1] *DCH*, II, pp. 453-54, gives the tentative translations of 'damask' or 'part of a bed.' Though there is a superficial resemblance in English between 'damask' and 'Damascus,' no evidence is available to support a connection in Hebrew between these two words.

power.[1] The witnesses are not called to bring further evidence against Israel, but to act as guarantors of the verdict being announced.

14. *'that on the day I punish Israel for his transgressions, I will punish the altars of Bethel, and the horns of the altar shall be cut off and fall to the ground.'*

The proclamation concerns a day of visitation coming on Israel (for the idiom, 'visit upon,' see the comment on 3:2). The specific visitation was to take place against the altars at Bethel. Many altars did exist throughout Israel and Judah, in addition to the central sanctuary. Hence, Elijah could complain to God that his altars were broken down (1 Kings 19:10: *mizb^{e}choteka*, 'your altars'). While Samaria was the national capital of the northern tribes in Amos' day, Bethel was the location of 'the royal sanctuary' (7:13, Heb. *bêt mamlâkâh*, lit. 'house [or temple] of the kingdom'). Bethel is noted in the historical record as being the place where Jeroboam set up a major worship centre (1 Kings 12:32; 13:2; 2 Kings 23:15). Rather than continuing as a worship centre, Bethel will cease to be so because the horns of the altar will be broken off and fall to the ground. The horns were projections on the corners of the altar, probably there in order that the sacrifices could be securely tied to it (see Psa. 118:27). A large sandstone altar discovered at Beersheba provides an excellent example of an altar with horns.[2] The horns were also what an asylum seeker grasped when seeking refuge (for examples see 1 Kings 1:49-53; 2:28-31). With the horns on the altar at Bethel broken off, the worship site would be desolate and unusable.

[1] The term 'LORD' or 'God of hosts' (for both forms were used) can have a variety of meanings. 'Hosts' can refer to the angels, the heavenly bodies, the armies of Israel, and even the universe. An excellent summary of the Old Testament usage is provided by J. E. Hartley in *TWOT*, 2, pp. 750-51.

[2] For information, see *ISBE*, vol. 1, p. 450. For further information and an illustration, see *IDBSupp*, pp. 93-95.

15. *'I will strike the winter house along with the summer house, and the houses of ivory shall perish, and the great houses shall come to an end,' declares the* LORD.

The concluding verse of this section contains a play on the Hebrew word for house. The place name Bethel (*bêt 'ēl*) means 'the house of God.' Twice in this verse the word 'house of' occurs, with plural forms also occurring twice ('houses of,' 'great houses'). This is a testimony to the wealth of the community in Amos' time. Both summer and winter houses existed, as well as ones with ivory decoration and ones of large proportion. The climate of Palestine has two seasons. The winter (*chóref*) is wet and cold, and the summer (*qáyits*) hot and dry. While 'winter' does not feature again in the book of Amos, 'summer' does in the later vision of ripe fruits (see the commentary on 8:1, 2). The opulence of the society was shown by the residences that were adapted to the climatic conditions and the abundance of ivory carvings which were so prominent that the houses could be called 'houses of ivory' (*bâtte shên*). The ivory would have been imported, and it was used as inlay in furniture (see the references to beds of ivory in 6:4, and to Ahab's ivory house, 1 Kings 22:39). The prophet's message was that the place called 'the house of God' was soon to be denuded of her houses when this divine visitation took place. All the pomp and display of Bethel's inhabitants will vanish, and even the altar itself, a place of refuge, will be no more. The final word, 'declares the LORD,' is another reminder that the message is not Amos' own, but the LORD's.

Application

What we have in this section is the judgment announced because of covenantal disobedience. Not all the features of a covenantal lawsuit appear, but clearly here we have the judgment expressed against Israel, and specifically against the political and religious capitals of Samaria and Bethel. It comes to a climax in verse 11, and then some of the consequences are spelt out in verses 12-15. This message should not have surprised people in Amos' day, for it is simply a reiteration of the threats that are in Leviticus 26 and Deuteronomy 28 (see especially Lev. 26:25-33 and Deut. 28:36, 37, 49-52). The prophets were not innovators, but merely proclaimed a message to their own day that had been given long before.

How gracious God was to his people! He sent prophet after prophet to them, but they would not repent and turn from their disobedience. In Israel they had come to present false worship at Bethel, and somehow thought that they were safe in their luxurious houses. Suddenly, judgment would come on them. The message is the same for us today. God is indeed long-suffering, not wanting any to perish. However, he warns us that the day of the Lord will come as a thief in the night (2 Pet. 3:9, 10). No one should presume on God's enduring gracious nature and long-suffering. The message in Hebrews 2:1-4 is always relevant: if we neglect the message that has come through angels and men, and attested by signs and wonders, 'how shall we escape if we ignore such a great salvation?'

2. *Failure to Repent (4:1-13)*

a. Condemnation of Socialites (4:1-3)

1. *'Hear this word, you cows of Bashan, who are on the mountain of Samaria, who oppress the poor, who crush the needy, who say to your husbands, "Bring, that we may drink!"'*

The opening call, 'hear this word,' would have awakened apprehension, as it was used already in 3:1 to introduce the denunciation of Israel as the chosen people of the covenant. Now the focus is especially on the women, called here 'cows of Bashan.' The territory of Bashan was east of the Sea of Galilee, part of the territory that was taken from Og at the time of the conquest. It was allotted to the half-tribe of Manasseh (Josh. 13:30; 21:6), and Golan was a city of refuge within that territory (Josh. 20:8). The cows are also said to be 'on the mountain of Samaria.' Clearly the expressions are pointing to the women of Israel. They are compared to the fat cattle of a well-known grazing area to highlight their luxurious situation, and are depicted calling for their husbands to bring them drink. The women are singled out for special attention because of their role in the subjugation of the poor. They oppressed the poor and crushed the needy. No maternal feelings were shown to those most in need of assistance.

2. *'The Lord GOD has sworn by his holiness that, behold, the days are coming upon you, when they shall take you away with hooks, even the last of you with fishhooks.'*

Again the Lord GOD speaks (see 3:13), this time pledging himself by solemn oath to act in judgment against these women. The contrast between their actions and those of God himself is made plain by the addition of the words 'by his holiness.' The women have been acting quite contrary to the provisions of the law and the needs of others, while God continues to act in accordance with his own nature. His righteous acts are a demonstration of his intrinsic holiness. The impending judgment is announced by saying, 'behold, days are coming upon you.' It is preferable to keep the word 'days' in translation here rather than paraphrase like the NIV rendering ('The time will surely come'). This is because it is an important term in the Old Testament teaching concerning God's ultimate judgment. The word 'behold' (Heb. *hinnêh*) serves to arrest attention, and to point decisively to the appointed judgment on these women. The threat is that they will be taken away, though the verb here is singular (*nissâ' 'et^ekem*, 'it will take you [pl.] away'). No subject is expressed, though in the context something like 'enemy' is implied. The judgment has traditionally been taken to mean that the women will be led out by [fish] hooks and their remnant with [fish] hooks. The introduction of the idea of fishing does not fit comfortably with the mention of cattle in the previous verse. Hence, other alternatives have to be considered. Since the second word for 'hook' in this verse (*sîr*) can mean a pot, it is plausible to suggest the word *tsinnâh* can denote a basket.[1] Thus, the warning is that the women will be involuntarily removed, being dragged out in suitable containers through restricted openings in the city walls. Probably the implication is that they will already be dead. It is the corpses that are going to be dragged out. Down to the very last of them, this divine judgment will, therefore, take effect. The expression, 'the last of you' (Heb. *'^acharît^eken*), could possibly mean 'your descendants,' which would be a future threat against posterity.

> 3. *'And you shall go out through the breaches, each one straight ahead; and you shall be cast out into Harmon,' declares the* Lord.

The future invasion of Samaria will result in the destruction of the fortified city so that breaches in the walls will become the way by which the women will be dragged away. The expression to go 'straight ahead' (Heb. *'ishshâh negdâh*) is parallel to the one in Joshua 6:5, 20, that describes how the Israelites rushed 'straight in' (*'ish negdâh*) when the walls of Jericho collapsed. The bodies are going to be 'cast out.' The verb used here (*shâlak*, ho.) is used elsewhere in the prophets, both for the throwing out corpses (see Isa. 34:3; Jer. 14:16), and also in connection with the exile (Jer. 22:28). It is possible that there is a mingling of two ideas here, both death and exile. Where the bodies will be taken to is unclear, as the word

[1] Cf. *DCH*, VII, p. 135.

'*Harmon*' does not occur anywhere else within the Old Testament. This has led to many suggested emendations,[1] the most plausible being that it is a variant of '*Hermon*.' If that is so, then the idea is that the devastation and removal of people would go at least as far north as Mount Hermon. The section ends with the usual confirmation that this is indeed the LORD's declaration of intent.

b. Sinful Worship (4:4, 5)

> 4. *'Come to Bethel, and transgress; to Gilgal, and multiply transgression; bring your sacrifices every morning, your tithes every three days.'*

The people as a whole are now addressed. The imperatives in verses 4, 5 are plural, and those spoken to are called 'Israelites' (lit. 'sons of Israel'). The command to go to Bethel and Gilgal is ironic, because it is quite clear that the prophet is accusing the people of false religious practice. More than that, the practices that they engage in are said to be futile. To continue as they are doing will only result in even more sinful actions! The words, 'transgress … and multiply transgression,' are typical of Hebrew poetry, where the thought in the first colon is increased greatly in the second. The words are from the same root (*pâsha'*), that means 'to rebel' or 'sin.' Bethel (Heb. *bêt-'ēl*, 'house of God') was in the territory of Ephraim, probably at modern Beitin, about 17 km (10.5 miles) north of Jerusalem. It was one of the sites where the ark of the covenant was located after the conquest, and where Jeroboam I, after the division of the kingdom, placed a golden calf in order to try and rival the temple at Jerusalem. Gilgal was a name given to several sites in Palestine,[2] but it is most likely that the one mentioned here was the site where Israel first encamped across the Jordan (Josh. 4:19). It was a strategic

[1] *DCH*, II, p. 593.

[2] For a good summary, see *NIDOTTE*, 4, pp. 683-85.

site with strong religious connections. 'Bring your sacrifices every morning, your tithes every three days' is a possible translation, but there are others.[1] It is especially the frequency of the tithes that is in question. The MT has *lishlóshet yâmîm*, 'every three days,' or, 'on the third day.' The former is more likely, as the context favours the idea of a profusion of offerings far in excess of what the law stipulated. Instead of three-yearly tithes (Deut. 14:28), the people were bringing them every three days!

5. *'offer a sacrifice of thanksgiving of that which is leavened, and proclaim freewill offerings, publish them; for so you love to do, O people of Israel!' declares the Lord* GOD.

Amos now confronts them with what they love to do (Heb., 'what you love'). But what they loved was far different from what the LORD loved. What they cared a great deal for, God cared nothing for. They brought leavened bread as a thank-offering, whereas the law specified that the grain offerings, as a thanksgiving and sacrifices of well-being, were to be with unleavened bread (Lev. 7:12, 13). Moreover, these should have been spontaneous offerings given by grateful worshippers. However, Amos tells them to make public their approach to the altar. They are called on to 'proclaim' and 'publish' about them (Heb. *qir^{e}'û*, 'proclaim,' and *hashmî'û*, 'make known'). Ostentatious display of ceremonial religion was what the people delighted in, without comparable heart religion. Once more a section ends with the certification that it is indeed a declaration of the Lord GOD.

Application

Throughout Scripture particular classes of people are singled out at times because of their sins. In verses 1-3 it is

[1] See T. J. Finley, *Joel, Amos, Obadiah*, pp. 205-7 for some of the possibilities.

wealthy women who come under condemnation. In the midst of all their feasting they didn't realise their danger, for Samaria would fall to invaders and they themselves would be taken out through gaps in the city wall. The warning to all of us is that if we think we are standing, we need to take heed lest we fall (1 Cor. 10:12). Pride and arrogance should have no place in our thinking when we approach God. Neither should mere formality in religious observances be considered a substitute for real religious experience. Each of us has to examine ourselves whether we are living in the faith (2 Cor. 13:5). No outward action can take the place of genuine heart religion.

c. Lessons Forgotten (4:6-9)

6. *'I gave you cleanness of teeth in all your cities, and lack of bread in all your places, yet you did not return to me,' declares the* LORD.

The focus is now on divine visitations in the past. The prophet is not depicting them as though they were simply natural disasters but as definite acts of God (see commentary on 3:6). Even though God had shown his sovereign power, no repentance had been shown by the people. The first statement is emphatic, with the pronoun 'I' (Heb. *'ᵃnî*) appearing in addition to the pronominal marker on the verb (*nâttatî*, 'I have put'). The expression, 'and I also gave cleanness of teeth' is a figurative expression for the lack of suitable food. This description of a famine situation is amplified in the following clause, 'and lack of bread in all your places.' Even then God's sovereign dealings with them did not result in their repentance. They did not return to him.[1] The identification of the speaker is clear from the concluding, 'declares the LORD.'

[1] The Heb. idiom is 'to return to,' with several different prepositions being used with the verb *shûv*: *'el*, *'ad*, *'al*, *lᵉ*, *bᵉ*. See *DCH*, VIII, pp. 281-82.

7. *'I also withheld the rain from you when there were yet three months to the harvest; I would send rain on one city, and send no rain on another city; one field would have rain, and the field on which it did not rain would wither.'*

The second affliction that had been visited upon Israel was drought, and it is introduced with the same emphatic declaration as in the previous verse: 'And also I (Heb. *'ânokî*, the longer form of the pronoun) withheld …' The LORD had withheld rain from them when the harvest was still three months away. Either the rain had not come, or else it had stopped prematurely. Both early and later rain were needed (see Deut. 11:14), the later rain particularly to produce good ears of grain.[1] In God's providential governance, one town had rain while another had not. The lack of moisture meant that the consequence was that the land dried up.

8. *'so two or three cities would wander to another city to drink water, and would not be satisfied; yet you did not return to me,' declares the LORD.*

Even such a divine visitation did not bring about a change of heart and mind among the people. They wandered from town to town, looking for satisfaction for their thirst, but there was no water available. Temporal deprivations had no effect on their spiritual life, other than to keep them obstinate towards God. The refrain, '"yet you did not return to me," declares the LORD,' brings the recurring message of hard hearts and stubborn wills that would not be moved by demonstrations of God's sovereign purposes.

9. *'I struck you with blight and mildew; your many gardens and your vineyards, your fig trees and your olive trees the locust devoured; yet you did not return to me,' declares the LORD.*

[1] For information on the rainy season in Israel, see Denis Baly, *The Geography of the Bible*, new and revised ed. (London: Lutterworth Press, 1974), pp. 47-51.

The third way in which God showed his displeasure was by destroying crops, attacking their 'gardens and vineyards.' He struck them 'with blight and mildew.' The word 'blight' (*shiddâfôn*) is used to describe the effect of a hot, dry wind that blows from the east, withering the plants within a day. 'Mildew' (*yêrâqôn*) only occurs six times in the Old Testament, and five of these cases, including this one, describe a disease that resulted in the failure of plants. The exact botanical identification is unclear. 'Your fig trees and your olive trees' did not escape either, as 'locusts devoured' them. The word used here for 'locusts' (*gâzâm*) only occurs here and in Joel 1:4 and 2:25. The LXX translated it by a word meaning 'caterpillar' (*kampê*). Most probably it is a reference to a locust at an immature stage. The picture presented is that all the productive agriculture had been lost. Famine was staring them in the face. God's longsuffering nature is shown by the fact that he repeatedly struck their crops as judgment in order to impel his people to examine their relationship with him. The threat of exile was not a hasty response of God (see 4:2, 3; 5:1-3). Even devastation of such magnitude did not bring about repentance, and hence the sorrowful verdict is repeated again: '"yet you did not return to me," declares the LORD.'

d. Failure to Repent (4:10, 11)

> 10. *'I sent among you a pestilence after the manner of Egypt; I killed your young men with the sword and carried away your horses, and I made the stench of your camp go up into your nostrils; yet you did not return to me,' declares the LORD.*

Just as God had displayed his sovereign power against Egypt by sending plagues, so had he inflicted his own people with similar visitations. The word used here for 'pestilence' (*déver*) is used in the biblical text regarding the pestilences in Egypt (Exod. 5:3; 9:3, 15), and it can refer to deaths of humans and animals. To be afflicted by the plague was one of the serious threats that God made against his people (Lev. 26:25). Bubonic plague was one of the most feared diseases in antiquity as it spread so rapidly and caused death so quickly. The climate in the Near East and the lack of sanitation made it a geographical area notorious for outbreaks of plague. Its spread may well have been linked at times with warfare, and Amos declares that God had killed their 'young men with the sword,' and 'carried away' their horses. This may be referring to the constant defeat in battle they had known, especially at the hands of the Syrians before the strong rule of Jeroboam II gave greater strength to Israel. The death of so many horses on the battlefield may well have accentuated the judgment that the plague inflicted. Even such terrible events did not cause the people to repent and turn to the LORD.

> 11. *'I overthrew some of you, as when God overthrew Sodom and Gomorrah, and you were as a brand plucked out of the burning; yet you did not return to me,' declares the LORD.*

What happened at Sodom and Gomorrah (Gen. 19:23-29) is often used in Scripture as a demonstration of God's anger being displayed against an unrepentant people. This is so for the New Testament as well as the Old Testament (see, in addition to this passage, Deut. 29:23; Isa. 1:9; Jer. 49:18; Lam. 4:6; Luke 17:29; 2 Pet. 2:6). The verb 'overthrew' (*hâpak*), while applied to God's judgment on Sodom and Gomorrah, is also used of God's promised treatment of Jerusalem (2 Kings 21:13), Nineveh (Jon. 3:4) and the unbelieving Gentiles (Hag. 2:22). It was not action against the whole population but against part of it, 'some of you' (Heb. *bâkem*),[1] a matter taken up later in the verse with reference to an escaped remnant. Some event that took place in Israel is compared to what happened to Sodom and Gomorrah. Not surprisingly, many have identified this event with

[1] This is most probably a partitive use of the preposition be. See *IBHS*, pp. 198-99.

an earthquake, and specifically with the earthquake mentioned in 1:1 by which Amos dates his prophecy. However, nothing in the context demands this identification, and as the verb 'overthrow' can signify various types of calamity it is probably best to look for something other than an earthquake. It could have been a military defeat, or perhaps this is a summary statement of many different adverse circumstances through which the nation passed. The covenantal curses listed in Deuteronomy 28 included drought (verses 23, 24), military conquest (verses 25, 26), locusts (verse 38), and famine (verses 47, 48). A number of these may have been in view. However, out of that situation a remnant escaped, called here 'a brand plucked out of the burning.' The expression (*kᵉ'ûd mutstsâl missᵉrêfâh*) is almost identical with the one in Zechariah 3:2 ('a brand plucked from the fire,' *kᵉ'ûd mutstsâl mê'êsh*). Both refer to a burning stick that is taken out of the fire, indicating a remnant were saved from the utter destruction that God brought upon the land. They are scorched and scarred, almost consumed, but nevertheless rescued by God's grace. Even such a divine intervention did not change the heart of the people, for persisting in their rebellion they did not return to the LORD.

e. A Meeting with God (4:12, 13)

> 12. *'Therefore thus I will do to you, O Israel; because I will do this to you, prepare to meet your God, O Israel!'*

The inevitable consequence of failure to show repentance was the announcement of impending judgment: 'Therefore thus I will do to you.' The declaration was even more alarming because it did not contain any specific information as to what 'thus' embodied. Seeing that there had been no repentance, the LORD threatened the people with unnamed afflictions. The message is reinforced by repetition of the main idea: 'I will do this to you, prepare to meet your God,' with still no amplification to spell out the coming disaster. This was an ominous development in the relationship that should have been startling enough to produce a change of heart. What was needed was preparation for defending themselves before their sovereign. His instruction is: 'Prepare to meet your God, O Israel.' The verb 'prepare' (Heb. *kûn*) is used in settings where people needed to get their hearts ready for appearing before God. No difference seems to exist between the usage here and other passages that specifically mention the heart (see 1 Sam. 7:3; 2 Chron. 12:14). Just as Israel had to prepare for meeting God on Sinai (Exod. 19:15), so Israel in Amos' day had to make due preparations for a decisive confrontation with him. In effect, this is a further call to the people to amend their ways, and also a further indication of divine grace that withholds judgment pending reformation.

> 13. *For behold, he who forms the mountains and creates the wind, and declares to man what is his thought, who makes the morning darkness, and treads on the heights of the earth—the* Lord*, the God of hosts, is his name!*

Accompanying the call for repentance is a declaration of God's sovereign power. Five aspects of his rule are expressed in hymnic style using participles:[1] 'forms,' 'creates,' 'declares,' 'makes,' 'treads.' These almost become divine titles. Anyone who meets God has to reckon with the creator of the mountains and the winds. Significantly, verbs are used that recall the account of creation in Genesis 1:2 (for 'forms' [*yôtsêr*], see Gen. 2:7, 8, 19; for 'creates' [*bôrê'*], see Gen. 1:1, 21, 27; 2:3; for 'makes' [*'osêh*], see Gen. 1:7, 11, 12, 16, 25, 26, 31). He also does not leave humans in darkness, but declares his will and purpose to them (see 3:7, he reveals 'his secret to his servants the prophets'). To say he 'declares to man what is his thought' is not

[1] Similar hymnic passages occur in another 8th-century BC prophet. See Isaiah 40:22-29; 44:24-28; 45:7, 18. This may well have been a poetic style of the period.

asserting universal revelation. It is simply an acknowledgement that revelation makes knowledge of the great creator possible. The word for 'thoughts' (*sêach*) only occurs here in the Old Testament, and while the suffix ('his') could refer to man, it suits the context better to follow the ESV. He is also said to be the one 'who makes the morning darkness.' While the opposite (creating light out of darkness) is the more common thought in the Old Testament, yet his power is seen in the ability to quench the strong light of dawn. The final clause declares that he 'treads on the heights of the earth.' This is ambiguous. It could refer to the high places that were the locations of worship, especially Canaanite. Alternately, it could refer to the mountains and hills, with the LORD being depicted in anthropomorphic language as striding over them. The context is dealing with God's creation and his rule over it, and hence it is best to take the alternative as the interpretation. The picture was a terrifying one for Israel. They had to make preparations to meet this God of might, the eternal creator, who was also their judge. The theophany Amos pictures reminds the reader of another 8th-century prophet, Micah, who depicts a similar theophany, that leads to the thought of judgment. This is reinforced by the use of an exalted title for God at the conclusion of the verse: 'the LORD, the God of hosts, is his name!' While 'LORD' has appeared many times already in Amos, this is the second occurrence of 'the God of hosts' that first appeared in 3:13 (see commentary).

Application

Warnings had been given repeatedly to Israel, but to no avail. The verdict is repeated five times: '"Yet you did not return to me," says the LORD' (verses 6, 8, 9, 10, 11). Their hearts became stubborn without the gracious intervention of the Holy Spirit. We need to pray for ourselves and others that God will give us softened hearts that will respond in obedience to his claims upon us. A contemporary of Amos, the prophet Hosea, challenged the people of Israel to demonstrate their obedience to the Lord:

> *Come, let us to the Lord our God*
> *with contrite hearts return:*
> *Our God is gracious, nor will leave*
> *the desolate to mourn.*
>
> *His voice commands the tempest forth,*
> *and stills the stormy wave;*
> *And though his arm be strong to smite,*
> *'tis also strong to save.*
>
> Scottish Paraphrase of Hosea 6:1.

3. *Indictment of an Unjust People (5:1-17)*

This is the third command with the same opening words (see 3:1; 4:1; 5:1), and it brings the message to a climax. It is addressed to the 'house of Israel,' whereas 3:1 was addressed to 'O people of Israel, against the whole family that I brought up out of the land of Egypt.' What is now different is that the prophet declares that he is lifting up 'a lamentation' against Israel. The Hebrew word for 'lament' (*qînâh*) is uniformly used of a song sung as a vocal expression of grief over the death of a person, or over the loss of a town. What is surprising here is that it is used of Israel *before* the final calamity has overtaken her. It is a very forceful way of depicting the complete destruction of Israel that was going to take place through enemy invasion. The use of this language is confirmation of the inevitability of Israel's devastation.

Echoes of the covenantal warnings given in Deuteronomy 28 seem to underlie several of the expressions in verses 1-11. The idea of 'going out' (verse 3; NIV 'marching out') resembles Deuteronomy

28:6, 19, while building houses and planting vineyards without being able to utilise them is close to Deuteronomy 28:30, 39.

A chiastic pattern helps to make the song even more memorable. This is the form that it takes:

A. *Lament over Israel* (verses 1-3)
B. *A call to repentance* (verses 4-6)
C. *The reason for God's judgment on Israel* (verses 7-13)
B. *A call to repentance* (verses 14, 15)
A. *Lament over Israel* (verses 16, 17)

a. Lament over Israel (5:1-3)

1. *Hear this word that I take up over you in lamentation, O house of Israel:*

No explanation is given of what is meant by 'lifting up' a lament against Israel. It could be that the voice was lifted up or that there was some visual placarding of the message. The word 'lament' (*qînâh*) is most frequently employed in the books of Jeremiah and Ezekiel. Here it is used to call attention graphically to the disaster that was going to overtake Israel. While 'house of Israel' is singular, the collective 'over you' is plural (*'ᵃlêkem*), directing the message to all within Israel.

2. *'Fallen, no more to rise, is the virgin Israel; forsaken on her land, with none to raise her up.'*

The message concerns 'virgin Israel,' who is depicted as 'fallen … with none to raise her up.'[1] In the Old Testament, royal cities were often referenced as though they were young women. While the plural,

[1] The idiom here is a common Hebrew way of denoting the idea of 'not again doing something' by use of the expression, 'she shall not add.' See *IBHS*, p. 656, 39.3.1b.

'daughters of Zion,' is a designation of women of Zion, the singular 'daughter of Zion' (or, if the words are in apposition, 'daughter Zion') is a designation of Jerusalem. Thus, 'daughter of Zion' is quite common as a term for Jerusalem (e.g., Isa. 1:8; 62:11; Jer. 6:2; Mic. 4:8), while 'virgin daughter of Zion' (Isa. 37:22) and 'virgin Babylon' (Isa. 47:1) also occur. The descriptive term used of the nation Israel, 'virgin Israel,' is also found in Jeremiah 18:13. She has been deserted, never again to rise. The use of the verb 'fall' (*nâfal*) often goes beyond the simple meaning of falling, for it also has a variety of military connotations such as falling in battle (Judg. 20:44), or falling by an opponent's hand (1 Chron. 20:8).[1] Self-help and other human assistance are both ruled out. The fall of Israel was going to be final, without the possibility of restoration.

> 3. *For thus says the Lord* G*OD: 'The city that went out a thousand shall have a hundred left, and that which went out a hundred shall have ten left to the house of Israel.'*

The message of the Sovereign LORD is that the towns and villages (Heb. *'îr* denotes a town of varying size, from the smallest hamlet to the greatest in extent and population) will be reduced to insignificant numbers—about a tenth in every case. When the deportation took place after the fall of Samaria in 722 BC, another 27,290 people were taken into exile, in addition to those already removed by Tiglath-pileser and Shalmaneser.

b. A call to repentance (5:4-6)

An example of intricate poetry occurs in these verses with a chiastic arrangement that stresses two place names, Bethel and Gilgal. Here is the pattern with the key words in bold font:

[1] I have discussed the usage of *nâfal*, including the military overtones, in *NIDOTTE*, 3, pp. 129-31.

4-6a. *This is what the* L*ORD* *says to the house of Israel:*

*'**Seek** me and **live**;*
*but do not seek **Bethel**,*
*and do not enter into **Gilgal**,*
or cross over to Beersheba;
*for **Gilgal** will surely go into exile,*
*and **Bethel** will be reduced to nothing.*
***Seek** the* L*ORD* *and **live**' (NRSV).*

Even at this late stage, the LORD extended a message of hope for the people, and this is emphasised by its repetition in verses 6 and 14. To 'seek the LORD' is to come to him with heartfelt longing and living trust. What is promised is 'life,' that stands in marked contrast to the fate of fallen Israel depicted in verses 2 and 3. Other prophets used the same type of language, encouraging the people to repent and return to the LORD (see Isa. 55:1-3).

5. The negative side of this call is the instruction not to seek Bethel, Gilgal, or Beersheba. As noted earlier (see commentary on 4:4), these places had clearly become sites of pagan worship. Bethel was the main sanctuary for the northern kingdom, established there with priests who were serving in the high places in order to discourage the people from taking any part in the worship in Jerusalem. As it was on the southern boundary of Israel, another major shrine centre was established at Dan in the north (1 Kings 12:25-33). Gilgal was the site on the western side of the Jordan where the Israelites first camped after crossing the river (Josh. 4:19), and clearly it became a place of particular significance for the people.[1] Beersheba was on the southern boundary of Judah's territory. A later reference in this book (8:14) even provides evidence that there was a pagan god known as

[1] Gilgal means 'a circle,' and more than one location was so named. See Deut. 11:30, where the Gilgal mentioned has to be much further south than 'the eastern border of Jericho' (Josh. 4:19).

'the god of Beersheba.' The Israelite's visits to these sites would have to be abandoned in order to show the reality of repentance. Continued presence at pagan sanctuaries would be utterly inconsistent with obedience to the living God.

The future of Gilgal is captivity. The site is personalised and the fact that people are going to be taken into captivity is described as being Gilgal's exile. The threat is made even more memorable for the alliteration and assonance it contains: *kî haggilgâl gâloh yigleh*, 'for Gilgal shall surely go into exile.' The fate of Bethel is not going to be any better, for it is to be reduced to nothingness.

> 6. *Seek the* L*ORD* *and live, lest he break out like fire in the house of Joseph, and it devour, with none to quench it for Bethel.*

The call to seek the LORD is repeated in a slightly altered form. Instead of 'seek me' (verse 4), the prophet now puts the command in the third person, 'seek the Lord, and live.' The repetition reinforces the compassion of God for his erring people. Judgment could only be averted if they listened to his word and obeyed it. As often in the Old Testament God's judgment is depicted as fire (e.g., Lev. 10:1-3; Num. 16:35; Ezek. 10:2), and in this case it will come sweeping through 'the house of Joseph.'

This is one of the alternative expressions for the northern tribes, as the sons of Ephraim were descendants of Joseph. The devouring fire will do its work without anyone being able to quench it. This is another indication of the inevitability of judgment for Israel. It will be all-consuming.

Application

> This passage, while describing the wretched condition of Israel in God's sight, yet holds out hope. The invitation is, 'Seek me and live' (verse 4), a call that is repeated twice

later in this chapter (verses 6 and 14). Mercy is held out to a wayward people. God's desire is 'that they should seek God, and perhaps feel their way toward him and find him. Yet he is actually not far from each one of us' (Acts 17:27). The gospel call continues to be a call to seek the Lord. The promise is that if we seek first his kingdom and his righteousness, then all other things will be added as well (Matt. 6:33). The last great prophet, the Lord Jesus, still calls in the gospel message for us to seek and find.

c. The Reasons for God's Judgment on Israel (5:7-13)

7-9. *O you who turn justice to wormwood and cast down righteousness to the earth! He who made the Pleiades and Orion, and turns deep darkness into the morning and darkens the day into night, who calls for the waters of the sea and pours them out on the surface of the earth, the* Lord *is his name; who makes destruction flash forth against the strong, so that destruction comes upon the fortress.*

The central part of this section comes to the heart of the problem in Israel, and also the consequences of the people's actions. They had universally failed to uphold 'justice' in the land, compared here to turning it into bitterness or throwing 'righteousness' to the ground. Verses 8 and 9 are marked off as a parenthesis in the NIV translation, as it identifies the one with whom they have to give account. He is the mighty God who has brought the universe into existence, and that includes the constellations like 'the Pleiades and Orion.' Both these words are rare. 'Pleiades' (*kîmâh*) only occurs three times (Job 9:9; 38:31; Amos 5:8), and, on each occasion, Orion (*kᵉsîl*) appears with it, while in Isaiah 13:10, Orion is used alone. Taking into account the early versions, these renderings in the ESV (and most English versions) are the best possible in the light of present knowledge. Israel is to remember that her God has such power that he even brought heavenly constellations such as Pleiades and Orion into being. He is also able to turn 'deep darkness into the morning.' The word for blackness (*tsalmâvet*) occurs 18 times in the Old Testament, all in poetry. The traditional rendering is 'valley of the shadow of death,' as in Psalm 23:4. Though this position has received strong support, an alternative, 'deep darkness,' has been proposed. In a context such as this, this latter rendering appears to make good sense.[1] No direct mention is made of death or dying in the passage, and hence the translation 'deep darkness' fits in well, especially with the parallel in the next phrase: 'and darkens the day into night.' The reference could be to a solar eclipse, or else just be a general expression relaying the truth that God is able to control all the forces of the natural world. He is also able to make 'the waters of the sea' become rain that waters 'the surface of the earth.' Israel's God was not to be confused with the gods of the Canaanites or any of the surrounding nations for 'the LORD is his name.' The covenantal God of Israel was indeed the God both of creation and providence. Moreover, he could destroy any man-made defensive structures such as 'the strong[hold]' and 'the fortress.' What might be impregnable to human forces could be brought to ruin by Israel's God.

10. *They hate him who reproves in the gate, and they abhor him who speaks the truth.*

After the parenthesis, the message reverts to the immediate state of the nation, and another accusation is made concerning the people: 'they hate him who reproves in the gate, and they abhor him who speaks the truth.' Abuse of the legal system was rampant in Israel. This subject has already been mentioned in 2:7 and it will appear again in 5:12, 18. 'In the gate' points to the fact that it was once the town entrance where legal procedures were carried out (see again in

[1] For this view, and a summary of other positions, see *NIDOTTE*, 3, pp. 807-10.

5:15, and see Deut. 21:19; Josh. 20:4; Ruth 4:1). No town centres as such existed in ancient Israel. Instead there was an open area of some size inside the gate that served as a market area, a court, and for civil administration. While the actual design of the gate area varied from place to place, yet it has been estimated that a typical area could accommodate about 800 to 1,000 people. Such squares have been excavated at Dan, Megiddo, Gezer, Beersheba, and Lachish.[1] The verb 'to reprove' (*yâkach*, hi.) is associated with legal actions, and here relates to the way in which someone sought to reprimand false doers in the legal forum, only to make himself/herself an object of hatred. Furthermore, truthful talking (*dovêr tâmîm*, lit. 'speaking sincerely') brought people into a detestable position, and the verb 'abhor' may also carry the connotation of exclusion.[2]

11. *Therefore because you trample on the poor and you exact taxes of grain from him, you have built houses of hewn stone, but you shall not dwell in them; you have planted pleasant vineyards, but you shall not drink their wine.*

The actions of the people are going to result in exile. Because they have acted harshly towards the poor they are not going to have the opportunity to enjoy their ill-gotten gains. A switch takes place in this verse in that the third-person verb of the previous verse is now replaced by a second-person: 'because *you* (second pers. pl. masc.) trample.' Such switches may seem strange to modern Western readers, but this type of change was typical of the ancient Near Eastern covenantal documents.[3] The meaning of the verb 'trample' is uncertain, as this is the only time that it occurs in the Hebrew Bible. It appears to be from a root that has this meaning (*bôs*, pol.).

[1] For full details on the gates of Israelite towns, see *TDOT*, 15, pp. 359-405, with detailed discussion on the Iron Age gates on pp. 383-86.

[2] So Ronald Youngblood in *TWOT*, 2, p. 976.

[3] The best discussion is by J. Niehaus, 'Amos,' pp. 420-21.

The LXX is quite different, rendering it 'they have smitten the poor with their fists,' which, though making sense in the context, does not rest on any substantial textual or linguistic evidence. The point being made is that the rich are able to build great mansions for themselves at the expense of the poor. These were made of stone, not the normal building material of sun-dried bricks (see Isa. 9:10). Their aggrandisement stands as a witness to their greed. However, another indication is given of the ultimate judgment that will befall Israel, though it is not spelt out fully until chapter 9. The consequences of the people's sins are now stated: 'you have built houses of hewn stone, but you shall not dwell in them; you have planted pleasant vineyards, but you shall not drink their wine.' They might 'enjoy the fleeting pleasures of sin' (in contrast to Moses, Heb. 11:25), but no long-term habitation of their houses will be possible, nor will they have the opportunity to drink wine made from the produce of their own vineyards. The word 'exile' is not used in this message, but clearly that is the outcome they have to expect (see the threats in Deut. 28:30, 38-40).

12. *For I know how many are your transgressions and how great are your sins—you who afflict the righteous, who take a bribe, and turn aside the needy in the gate.*

Nothing could be hidden from God's eyes; all was open to him, for even the darkness was as light to him (Psa. 139:12). The multitude of Israel's 'transgressions' and 'sins' were known to him. No great distinction is to be made between these words. The first, 'transgressions' (*pesha'*), refers to acts of rebellion against God, while the second, 'sins' (*chattā'ôt*) is the broadest Old Testament term for sin. Once more the focus is on abuse of the legal system. The expression 'how many are your transgressions and how great are your sins' has been translated in many different ways.[1] The

[1] For a summary of the various translations, see *NIDOTTE*, 3, p. 491.

combined expression may denote that not only were the actions many in number, but that they were pursued vigorously against the poor. Those who should have been clear of legal action because of their integrity, 'the righteous,' are ones who are oppressed, while bribery was a way of life for the oppressors. The 'needy' were left without any recourse to legal action to sustain their claims.

13. *Therefore he who is prudent will keep silent in such a time, for it is an evil time.*

The final verse in this section is introduced by the word 'therefore' (*lâkên*), a particle that often introduces judgment sayings in Amos (see 4:12; 5:11, 16; 6:7). The sentence, 'he who is prudent will keep silent in such a time,' is difficult because of three translational problems. The first one is the subject, 'the prudent man.' This represents a participle of a verb (*sâkal*, hi.) that means to demonstrate insight or knowledge, though sometimes it means to act with religious devotion. Perhaps the word 'pious' comes close to it. Secondly, the verb that the ESV translates as 'keeps silent' comes from a Hebrew root *d-m-m*, but several verbs share these same consonants.[1] Many translations have followed the AV that rendered it 'keep silence' (see RSV, NASB, NRSV, NEB, NLT), though some other renderings would fit the context, e.g. 'to weep.' In the absence of strong evidence to the contrary, it is best to retain something close to the AV translation. Thirdly, 'in such a time' is a paraphrase of the Hebrew that says, 'for it is an evil time' (*kî 'êt râ'âh hî'*). The exact phrase occurs also in Micah 2:3 where it denotes a time of calamity or distress, and that fits the context here. Putting these comments into a coherent position, the message is that in times of great distress it may be best for the pious person to

[1] *DCH*, II, pp. 450-52 lists five different verbs that all have the same three consonants. The meanings listed are 'be silent, cease,' 'weep,' 'moan, whisper,' 'maltreat, destroy, break, crush,' and 'level.'

keep quiet. The reason for this could be twofold: on the one hand, expression of truth will not be tolerated in such times, but, on the other hand, the advice could point to the fact that there comes a time when no words will alter the prevailing situation but may well draw unwelcome attention on the speaker.[1]

Application

> This section in Amos highlights a perennial problem for believers. The church is placed in a world that is distorted because of sin. Decisions in society are often made in order to achieve outcomes that will enhance the position or wealth of particular people. The abuse of due legal process, of which Amos speaks, is not foreign to modern society. Even though the Song of Moses had spoken of the lack of understanding that would prevent the people from realising where the nation was heading (Deut. 32:28, 29), in Amos' day they still were blind to the future. The same issues he was confronting are with us today, and the sickness of society is displayed in intolerance of what is good, and true, and just. The righteous must always be prepared to stand up for what is true.

d. Encouragement to Live (5:14, 15)

The people had come to a point of crisis. They have had to repent and turn to the LORD, or else continue on their sinful ways and remain under God's judgment. Just as Moses challenged Israel in his day to choose life and live (Deut. 30:19, 20), so Amos passes on to Israel in his day a similar message.

[1] J. A. Motyer, *The Day of the Lion: The Message of Amos* (London: Inter-Varsity Press, 1974), p. 115, suggests another interpretation. He takes the subject, 'the prudent man,' to mean 'someone who wants to get on.' This leads to the view that such a person would not speak in a particular situation because it may spoil his future prospects. While possible, this position seems remote from the context here.

14. *Seek good, and not evil, that you may live; and so the LORD, the God of hosts, will be with you, as you have said.*

The message is direct and plain: 'Seek good, and not evil, that you may live.' To 'seek' has the general idea of inquiring about, or acquiring knowledge, and here it implies, 'seek to know what is good' (see its use already in verse 4). Life would continue in the good land if the people shunned evil. The effect of that would be that the claim that they made ('the LORD is in our midst') would be a reality, not a false assertion on their part. The use of '*the God of hosts*' gives greater solemnity to the charge.

15. *Hate evil, and love good, and establish justice in the gate; it may be that the LORD, the God of hosts, will be gracious to the remnant of Joseph.*

The attitude towards evil has to be hatred of it, something conveyed elsewhere in the Old Testament (e.g., Psa. 97:10; Prov. 8:13). The verb 'love' can be used with the opposites, good and evil. Men can love evil (Psa. 52:3), but here the positive instruction is given to 'love good.' The theme of valid administration of justice is again the focus, as attitudes to good and evil are displayed in the manner in which justice is carried out in any society. Enough has been said earlier in this book about false justice to allow the prophet to pick up immediately the thought of the valid application of legal principles at the town gate (see the comment on verse 10).

e. Prosperity Lost (5:16, 17)

The condemnatory words of a prophet like Amos were bad enough in themselves. However, a threat was held out that the LORD himself would pass through the land, not in mercy but in judgment. The prophet puts this in a context in which all classes of society are joining together in mourning.

16. *Therefore thus says the* L*ORD*, *the God of hosts, the Lord: 'In all the squares there shall be wailing, and in all the streets they shall say, "Alas! Alas!" They shall call the farmers to mourning and to wailing those who are skilled in lamentation, and in all vineyards there shall be wailing, for I will pass through your midst,' says the* L*ORD*.

The inevitability of punishment is made plain by the opening word, 'therefore' (*lâkên*), that introduces the divine judgment. The combination of titles for God, 'the Lord, the God of hosts,' reinforces the solemnity of the rebuke. The message is that such a calamity is coming on the land that 'In all the squares there shall be wailing and in all the streets.' The word for 'wailing' (*mispêd*) is commonly used in connection with some disastrous event (see Jer. 48:38; Ezek. 27:31; Mic. 1:8, 11). The word for 'alas' (*hô*) only occurs here in the Old Testament, and is probably just a shortened variant of *hôy* (as in verse 18). The picture is of town squares, normally just inside the main gate, and streets resounding with anguished cries from the inhabitants. Summoning the farmers 'to mourning and to wailing those who are skilled in lamentation' reflects upon the mourning rituals in place at that time. It is unclear, however, what the implication of summoning the farmers is. The Hebrew word used here for 'farmer' (*'ikkâr*) probably denotes employed shepherds or agricultural workers rather than farm owners. The call is to go to those living and working outside of the city walls and bid them come and join in the mourning. Those people who are 'skilled in lamentation' (*yodᵉʿê nehî*, lit. 'those skilled in mourning') appear to have been a professional class who performed various rituals. It is unclear whether they were paid for their services. The word used for 'lamentation' (*nehî*) is not the usual word used in contexts such as this. Rather, it appears five times in Jeremiah (four of them in chap. 9, verses 10, 17, 18, 19, and also in the passage dealing with Rachel,

31:15), and in Micah 2:4. All these occurrences are in passages in which there is the threat of destruction to the land by warfare.

17. *'and in all vineyards there shall be wailing, for I will pass through your midst,' says the* L*ORD.*

This verse continues the thought of days of mourning that are going to be experienced by Israel. The wealth of the land is again in focus, with the reference to 'vineyards.' The opulence of the people is not going to be a means by which they will escape the impending calamity, for all will be involved. The explanation is introduced by the word 'for' (*kî*). Public lamentation will be the acknowledgement of divine judgment upon the land. This is emphasised by the use of the LORD's words: 'I will pass through your midst.' These words should have evoked dread in their hearers, for the expression is exactly the one used of God's 'passing through' (*'âvar*) the land of Egypt on the night of the first Passover (Exod. 12:12). Those who belonged to Israel were placed in exactly the same position as Egypt was, not as objects of mercy but as recipients of God's judgment. The final words of the verse, 'says the LORD,' were another reminder that the people were not dealing simply with the words of a prophet, but those of the LORD himself.

Application

Amos was not alone among the prophets in calling upon the people to seek the LORD. Isaiah told those of his day to 'seek the Lord while he may be found; call upon him while he is near' (Isa. 55:6). As in Amos, the implication was that the LORD may not always be ready to answer. But here Amos is telling those of his day that life depended on following God's ways, as doing so would be evidence of their hearts being set on him and his demands. Past history is called upon to reinforce their need for repentance, as what happened in Egypt at the time of the exodus (see 4:10 and 5:17) should have been a powerful warning. Recollection of days of God's favour should encourage people to listen to his call, especially when days of visitation upon sin are threatened. If 'every transgression or disobedience received a just retribution, how shall we escape if we neglect such a great salvation?' (Heb. 2:2, 3). That message must be heeded.

4

Announcement of the Exile (5:18–6:14)

1. *Unexpected Judgment (5:18-20)*

The message of Amos now reaches new heights, for he sets out to disabuse the people of a wrong concept of God. They thought that a day was coming in which God's favour and blessing would be apparent to all, as if the brightness of his glory were to shine over the land. Instead, Amos says, their religious rituals will not save them from God's wrath, and the inevitable end of the nation will be 'exile beyond Damascus' (5:27).

> 18. *Woe to you who desire the day of the LORD! Why would you have the day of the LORD? It is darkness, and not light.*

The theme of woe already spoken of in verse 16 is further enlarged, and this is done in a very dramatic way by the sudden introduction of the concept of 'the day of the LORD.' No explanation is given concerning the phrase, but the implication is that it was a known idea, and, therefore, mention of it would bring no surprise to Amos' hearers. This means that there was pre-prophetic eschatology that included this teaching, and the prophets in this period of Israel's history (8th century BC) were able to refer to it, while correcting their hearers' and readers' false understanding concerning it. The phrase itself, 'day of the Lord,' can be interpreted in various ways. When compared with the phrase, 'the day of Midian' (Isa. 9:4), it is quite possible that it had a military ring to it, 'the day monopolised by Jehovah as his day of victory.'[1] While in Amos the main thought is that evil will be swept away and judgment meted out to a sinful people, in Isaiah the concept is used in relation to the destruction of idols. In the Old Testament this special 'day' is related to a time when judgments will be inflicted on Israel (see, in addition to Amos 5:18, 20, Joel 1:15; 2:1, 11, 31; Zeph. 1:7, 14), but also on other nations (see Isa. 13:6; Ezek. 30:3; Joel 3:14; Obad. 15). That is to say, 'the day of the Lord' in the Old Testament is spoken of as taking place *within* the Old Testament era, whereas in the New Testament 'the day of the Lord' refers to the final day of judgment (1 Cor. 5:5; 1 Thess. 5:2; 2 Pet. 3:10).

Amos' expression at the opening of verse 18 relates to his sense of the doom awaiting those in Israel who long for the day of the Lord. They may earnestly desire the coming of that day,[2] but he raised the question as to its purpose: 'Why would you have the day of the Lord?' The syntax of this question is unusual. Literally it reads, 'Why this to (or, for) you, the day of the Lord?' The addition of 'this' can be explained as it is used at times with an interrogative to add emphasis to a question.[3] The best way to explain the remainder of the question is that the verb in the first statement ('long for') has

[1] Geerhardus Vos, *Biblical Theology: Old and New Testament*, p. 292. Elmer Martens, *God's Design: Focus on Old Testament Theology*, 2nd ed. (Grand Rapids: Baker Books, 1994), p. 132, quotes this definition approvingly in his survey of interpretation of 'the day of the Lord' (pp. 130-36). See also Martens' other discussion, 'Day of the Lord, God, Christ,' *Evangelical Dictionary of Biblical Theology*, ed. Walter Elwell (Grand Rapids: Baker Book House, 1996), pp. 146-49.

[2] The verb for 'long for' (*mit'avvîm*, hitp. part. masc. pl. of *'âvâh*) does not seem to carry any reflexive connotation, but rather is virtually an intensive form of the pi. stem of the same verb. See W. R. Harper, *A Critical and Exegetical Commentary on Amos and Hosea*, p. 131: 'Not the hypocritical Hithpôêl = pretend that they desire; nor the simple Pi'êl = desire, with the reflexive sense, desire for themselves; but earnestly desire and expect.'

[3] For this usage, see *DIHG-S*, p. 6, Rem. 3.

to be understood as the verb of the following statement. This type of ellipsis or gapping is fairly common in Hebrew poetry.[1] The answer that Amos gave must have startled his hearers: 'It is darkness, and not light.' The Hebrew construction (*v^{e}lo'-'ôr*) marks out 'light' as being the opposite of 'darkness,' not that 'there is no light.'[2] The use of the negative particle (*lo'*) before a noun such as 'night' is a way in which Hebrew forms compound expressions, rather like the addition of the English prefixes 'un-' and 'in-.'[3] Whatever the people were expecting the day of the LORD to be, they represented it as being 'light.' Now their hopes were dashed as the prophet told them of the overwhelming darkness that was coming. But something more seems intended here. Reference was made in verse 17 to the use of the expression 'I will pass through your midst,' that echoed the use of this phrase in the Exodus experience. Now another expression, 'darkness,' is picked up from that same period in Israel's history. God brought supernatural darkness on Egypt in the ninth plague (Exod. 10:21, 22; Psa. 105:28), while the pillar of fire and cloud darkened the way of the Egyptians and lit up the way for Israel (Exod. 14:20). What had been the experience of the Egyptians is now threatened to be that of Israel—'darkness and not light.' Judgment on Israel will resemble the judgment on Egypt.

> 19. *as if a man fled from a lion, and a bear met him, or went into the house and leaned his hand against the wall, and a serpent bit him.*

To illustrate the inevitability of God's judgment two illustrations are given, both with the implication that those at ease and in a relaxed state will suddenly be confronted with great danger. A

[1] *DIHG-S*, p. 163, §132.

[2] This would have required *v^e'ên 'ôr*.

[3] Other examples in Hebrew are 'a no-god' (*lo' 'êl*, Isa. 10:15) and 'a son not-wise' (*bên lo' châkâm*, Hos. 13:13). See further *DIHG-S*, p. 142, §116 (d).

man may escape from a lion, only to meet with a bear. Both lions and bears were native to Palestine in Old Testament times, and both were extremely dangerous. Escaping one danger was only a prelude to a greater danger. In a similar way, a man may reach the security of his own house, only to find that when he leans on the wall, a snake attacks him.[1] Pictorial representation of the coming judgment reinforces the threats already given by Amos.

20. *Is not the day of the* L*ORD* *darkness, and not light, and gloom with no brightness in it?*

The message given in verse 18 is reinforced by repetition and expansion. The first part of the question repeats the assertion of verse 18, while the second part uses parallel expressions to press home the point. The people in Israel were expecting light, only to find that the day of the LORD would be darkness. Though expecting brightness, they would be surprised by thick darkness.[2] The word for 'gloom' only occurs here in the Old Testament, but its meaning is clear because of the context, and also because of the use elsewhere of related words (*'ofel* and *'ᵃfêlâh*) that come from the same root (*'-f-l*).

Application

Right from the beginning of human existence men and women have challenged God's declarations. Amos was telling those in his day that their misunderstanding of future events was going to be put right. What they expected and what God was going to do were completely opposed to each

[1] Three times in this verse the Heb. definite article is used before 'lion,' 'bear' and 'snake.' However, in English the indefinite article is required. These are illustrations of how the article in Heb. may be used to designate a class, and normally the singular is used as here. See further, *DIHG~S*, p. 28, §31 (c).

[2] The Hebrew expression for 'without a ray of brightness?' (*vᵉlo' nogah lô*) is of the same type as 'and not light' in verse 18. See p. 91, n.2.

other. It is part of Satan's work to blind 'the minds of the unbelievers, to keep them from seeing the light of the gospel of the glory of Christ, who is the image of God' (2 Cor. 4:4). An important part of gospel proclamation is to correct hearers concerning their false understanding of God and his purposes. Sinful human ideas have to be replaced with godly wisdom that points us to the things of God. Amos' challenge to those of his day is replicated time and time again as the truth is made known.

2. *False Worship and Its Consequences (5:21-27)*

Passages such as this help us understand the practice of religion in Old Testament times. Since there is a restricted amount of information regarding how Israel actually carried out the Mosaic laws relating to worship, prophetic passages like this aid our understanding. They depict the original intent of God, alongside the abuse of his prescribed forms of worship. For a disobedient people, the only outcome was exile from their land, and that to a location far away, 'beyond Damascus' (5:27).

21. *'I hate, I despise your feasts, and I take no delight in your solemn assemblies.'*

God's attitude to the practices at that time, especially the feast days, was one of hatred. He had no pleasure in the way in which the people were altering the prescribed worship to fit their own ideas: 'I hate, I despise your feasts, and I take no delight in your solemn assemblies.' No great difference is to be seen in the two verbs, 'hate' (*sânê'*) and 'despise' (*mâ'as*). Combined, they describe the revulsion of God to what purported to be worship. The 'feasts' were probably the three main pilgrimage feasts—the Passover, the Feast of Weeks, and the Feast of Tabernacles. The Hebrew word for such a feast, *chag*, has as its parallel *hajj* in Arabic. The 'assemblies' may well have been the closing festival of such occasions. 'I take no delight' represents the Hebrew 'I do not smell,' though this verb is used, as per the rendering of the ESV, to have the metaphorical meaning of 'delight in.' With the negative particle as here, it is synonymous with 'hate' and 'despise.'

22. *'Even though you offer me your burnt offerings and grain offerings, I will not accept them; and the peace offerings of your fattened animals, I will not look upon them.'*

Not only were the festive assemblies in Israel unacceptable to the LORD, but also the sacrifices that the people offered. Three particular sacrifices are mentioned here. The first is the burnt offering (*'olâh*). This type of sacrifice was not practised in the Mesopotamian cults, but it was among the Canaanites. However, there was no strict parallel between Canaanite and Israelite usage, as only in Israel was the blood sprinkled on the altar. It is also referred to as 'the complete offering' (*kâlîl*), and, because it was offered daily, the term 'continual' (*tâmîd*) was applied to it as well (see Exod. 29:42; Num. 4:16; Deut. 8:11). The second offering is 'the grain offering' (*minchâh*) that consisted of cereals, whether dry, crushed, or baked in cakes (see Lev. 2:1-16 and 6:14-23 [Hebrew text, verses 7-16][1] for details). The third offering is 'the peace offering' (*shélem*). Part of it was burnt on the altar, but the rest was shared by the priests and the worshipper. The term occurs almost ninety times in the Old Testament, and in every case but this one it appears in the plural form. Several views have been propounded regarding its significance, but the best is that it represented the communion or fellowship between the offerers and God.[2] This message does not appear to be

[1] Long before the present versification of the text of the Old Testament existed, another system was in place. It differed at some places from the one later adopted and seen in our English Bibles. This passage in Lev. 6 displays this variation.

[2] For a summary of views relating to the significance of this sacrifice, see *TWOT*, II, pp. 930-32.

disallowing sacrifice, but rather pointing to God's attitude towards insincere worship. His declaration, through his servant Amos, is that he 'will not accept them' and 'will not look upon them,' both terms pointing to failure on the part of his worshippers to present their offerings with a right spirit and attitude.

23. *'Take away from me the noise of your songs; to the melody of your harps I will not listen.'*

While no prescription was given in the law relating to music in connection with the offering of sacrifice, yet it appears that, on occasion, music was associated with religious ritual, as well as on other occasions (see Amos 6:5). Here 'songs' and 'the melody of your harps' are both displeasing to God, perhaps because they were both so alien to the intent of the sacrificial system. What the people thought of as music was only a din to the LORD's ears. Revelry could not take the place of true religious devotion. God's word is that the songs will be banished, while he will refuse to listen to the harp music.

24. *'But let justice roll down like waters, and righteousness like an ever-flowing stream.'*

The message reverts now to a theme that had been expressed earlier, namely the injustices being practised throughout the nation (see 2:6-8; 5:6-13). God's desire is that 'justice' will 'roll down like waters, and righteousness like an ever-flowing stream.' The verb 'roll' (*gâlal*, ni.) is used virtually in the sense of 'flow,' and the syntax suggests a contrast is being drawn with what immediately precedes.[1] At times the imagery of water is utilised in the Old Testament to depict abundance. Thus, in Isaiah 48 the assurance is given that if due attention had been paid to God's commands, 'your peace would have been like a river, and your righteousness like the waves of the sea' (Isa. 48:18). The use of

[1] The construction at the opening of this verse is a simple vav with a ni. impf. of the verb *gâlal*, and this gives something of a contrast: 'But let ...'

the parallel expressions 'justice' and 'righteousness' follows the earlier use in verse 7.

25. *'Did you bring to me sacrifices and offerings during the forty years in the wilderness, O house of Israel?'*

This and the following verse are probably the most difficult in the book of Amos. Various views have been suggested.[1] Some have wanted to stress the object of the verb, 'me' (Heb. *lî*, 'to me'), but the grammar is against that as the emphasis falls on 'sacrifices and offerings' (*z^e^bâchîm ûminchâh*). The verse commences with the normal question marker (*ha-*), and it is the type that requires a 'yes/no' answer. Some questions of this kind are virtually exclamations, and this may be so here as well.[2] But the expected answer to the question is the negative, 'No!', and the problem is how to reconcile this with other passages in the Old Testament that suggest that Israel did bring sacrifices and offerings to the LORD during the desert wanderings. The Mosaic sacrificial system presupposed residency in the land of Canaan. Hence, its provisions pointed forward to a time when agriculture and animal husbandry would be the source of sacrificial offerings. Clearly some sacrifices were offered in the wilderness (see Exod. 18:12, regarding those brought by Jethro; and Lev. 9:8-24 regarding various offerings: sin and burnt offerings, peace offerings, and grain offerings, with Aaron as the responsible priest). However, the full sweep of sacrifices were not offered during Israel's time in the wilderness, and so the answer to the question has to be 'No.' Jeremiah 7:22, 23 has been appealed to in relation to this verse. There reference is made to the fact that on the day that the LORD brought Israel out of Egypt he did not give commands to them concerning the details of burnt offerings and sacrifices. The detailed prescriptions for sacrifice came later at Sinai.

[1] For a summary, see Billy K. Smith, 'Amos,' *Amos, Obadiah, Jonah* (NAC: Nashville: Broadman & Holman, 1995), pp. 113-15.

[2] See *IBHS*, pp. 684-85, §40.3b.

26. *'You shall take up Sikkuth your king, and Kiyyun your star-god—your images that you made for yourselves.'*

Like the previous verse, this one has also called forth various explanations.[1] Some have taken the first verb, 'take up' (*nâsâ'*) as a future, to go along with the future, 'I will send you into exile,' in verse 27. Others have considered this to be a conditional clause that is continued in the following verse: 'if you carry ... I will take you ...' It has also been suggested that the opening verb has to be taken as a past tense, and the clause forms a negative answer to the previous verse: 'No! But you carried ...' There is still another possibility and that is to take the verse as another question like verse 25, and that would expect a negative answer. Of these possible interpretations the third one has the least objections to it, and should be followed.

However, that still leaves questions about the remainder of the verse, and in particular the understanding of phrases like 'You shall take up Sikkuth your king,' 'your images that you made for yourselves,' and 'Kiyyun your star god.' That these phrases have created difficulty from an early period is clear from the LXX rendering of the verse: 'And you took up the shrine of Moloch, and the star of your god Ræphan, the images of them that you made for you yourselves.' This textual tradition, that differs from the MT, is followed in Stephen's speech as recorded in Acts 7:42, 43, with the additional alteration of the name 'Ræphan' to 'Remphan.'[2] Modern translations continue to show considerable variety in their renderings of this verse. The NIV translators recognised a problem with the words they translated as 'shrine' (*siccût*) and 'pedestal' (*kêvân*), and in a marginal note they indicated that these words could be names of Assyrian gods, Sakkut and Kaiwan. While this proposal has some

[1] The best list is probably provided by E. Hammershaimb, *The Book of Amos: A Commentary*, pp. 92-94.

[2] Both the LXX and NT manuscripts show considerable variation in regard to this name. It can be Raiphan, Remphan, Romphan, Rempha[n], Rompha, and Rephan.

attraction, yet it also faces difficulties. It would mean that in Amos' time the people were worshipping Assyrian gods, something that is not confirmed elsewhere. In addition, both Sakkut and Kaiwan were names associated with the worship of Saturn, and such repetition seems very unusual. Rather, it is best to stay with the text of the ESV or something similar.

The description given relates to forms of substitute worship for genuine worship of Israel's God. Such worship involved a shrine of their 'king,' i.e. their god, the pedestals on which idols were placed, and the star of their god. The latter is such an unusual expression, that some translations even omit it (see REB). The attempt to render it as 'your star-god' is unsupported by Hebrew grammar. Tentatively, it can be understood to be an ensign, such as was carried before kings.[1]

Two final comments on this verse help to tie together the interpretation. The first concerns the expression, 'You shall take up Sikkuth your king.' The verb 'to take up' (*nâśâ'*) can be used of carrying something around, and this fits the context here admirably. Biblical and extra-biblical evidence exist of the practice of carrying idols around in procession.[2] Isaiah makes the emphatic point that God carries his people, not the opposite as was the case with the Babylonians, who loaded their idols on to carts (Isa. 46:1-4). The second thing is the emphasis on the Israelites' worship degenerating into that of man-made idols. The accusation against them is that they had carried about these idols, 'that you made for yourselves.' Self-made gods were lifeless objects. The covenantal God of Israel did whatever pleased him; the idols lacked all the abilities that he possessed (Psa. 115:2-8). Amos' message was that just as the people were wrong in their understanding of the day of the LORD, so were they wrong in their basic assumptions regarding true worship.

[1] This is suggested in *DCH*, IV, p. 371.

[2] See *ANEP*, fig. 305, 535.

27. *'and I will send you into exile beyond Damascus, says the* L*ORD,' whose name is the God of hosts.*

The coming of the day of the LORD for Israel is announced as being the result of the nation's sin: '"and I will send you into exile beyond Damascus," says the LORD, whose name is the God of hosts.' 'Therefore' is simply the Hebrew conjunction (*v*[e]), but in this construction (*vav* consec. + perf.) it denotes the consequences of Israel's sins.[1] The judgment will take the form of the application of one of the covenantal curses: 'The LORD will bring you and your king whom you set over you to a nation that neither you nor your fathers have known' (Deut. 28:36; see also verses 64-68; 29:28). 'Beyond Damascus' could only mean one thing for those of Amos' time—Assyria, for no other power then would want to deport them in that direction. Damascus was the compass point to the north-east, and from there the trade routes led into the so-called Fertile Crescent. The people were not going to be taken to near neighbours. Rather, they were going far away. The warnings already given by Amos of banishment away from Palestine (see 3:12; 4:2, 3; 5:3, 11, 12) are now intensified, with specification of the future location of exiled Israel. The warning ends with a declaration that this message is indeed from the LORD, 'whose name is the God of hosts' (*'[e]lôhê hatsts[e]vâ'ôt sh[e]mô*). This is the same designation of God as in 4:13, that carries the reminder that he is the God of power, who is well able to fulfil the threats he has made against his people.

Application

This passage calls forth two observations. The first is how easily the human mind conjures up ways in which to attempt to worship God by the use of idols. It was so in Amos' day, just as it was in Moses', when the people in their

[1] See *DIHG-S*, p. 88, §71 (e).

rebelliousness of heart (lit. stiff-necked) made an idol while he was still on Mount Sinai with God (Exod. 32:7-20). In the prophetic summary of the reasons leading to the fall of the northern kingdom, mention is made explicitly of the rebelliousness of the people. They were like those long before, who, in imitation of the nations around them, 'went after false idols and became false' (2 Kings 17:15). Similarly, Ezra, after the return from exile, recalled that the same rebelliousness led to idolatry (Neh. 9:16-18). One mark of sinful minds is the capacity to exchange 'the glory of the immortal God for images made to look like mortal man and birds and animals and reptiles' (Rom. 1:23; see Psa. 106:20 and Hos. 4:7). The prayer of William Cowper (1731–1800) is ever relevant:

The dearest idol I have known,
Whate'er that idol be,
Help me to tear it from thy throne,
And worship only thee.

'O For a Closer Walk with God.'

The second observation is that abuse of the most solemn religious observances can easily occur. Amos' message earlier was a challenge to the people over their sinning while they worshipped at Bethel or Gilgal (4:4). Here it is the substitution of idols in place of their God. So too the church in Corinth had to be rebuked by Paul because of the abuse of the Lord's Supper. The people worshipping at Corinth were making the Lord's Supper an occasion for satisfying their hunger and thirst, something that they should have done at home (1 Cor. 11:20-22). Instead of being a blessing, their observance brought judgment on themselves (1 Cor. 11:27-34). True worship must be in spirit and in truth, following God's own directions for it.

3. *Declaration of punishment against those living in luxury (6:1-7)*

Attention now switches to the complacency of many in Israel and also Judah. While the kingdom was divided after Solomon's death, yet strictly speaking 'Israel' comprised the whole twelve tribes. Amos, from the south (Judah), in this passage includes condemnation of fellow southerners who lived in Jerusalem. Having addressed the wealthy women of Samaria already (see comments on 4:1-3), attention is now directed to wealthy and prominent men who are living very materialistic lifestyles without any sense of insecurity.

> 1. *'Woe to those who are at ease in Zion, and to those who feel secure on the mountain of Samaria, the notable men of the first of the nations, to whom the house of Israel comes!'*

The message to the complacent starts with a familiar interjection, 'woe' (*hôy*), that occurs over fifty times in the prophets, of which forty involve negative messages (Isa. 55:1 is an exception, where *hôy* introduces a positive invitation). It is directed to those 'who are at ease in Zion, and to those who feel secure on the mountain of Samaria.' The message relates to those in both Israel and Judah who share the same character. Clearly the terms are used in parallel—'ease' and 'feel secure.' The first of these relates to people who were not heeding the warning signs, or the messages delivered by Amos and other prophets. They could not comprehend that they might be in danger. Those in the northern kingdom were feeling secure. The verb used to describe them is that they were 'trusting' (*bâtach*) in the hill of Samaria. Their problem was one of false confidence. Both Zion and Samaria were elevated, and hence provided some physical barrier to invading armies. However, the main sin of the people was trusting in their physical location rather than in the LORD. They failed to heed the directions that they had been given to trust in him (Psa. 4:5; 37:3; Isa. 26:4). Their complacency also encouraged them to vaunt their own national interests to such an extent that they thought theirs was the foremost nation. The leaders, 'the notable men,' were influential in the nation, and probably others came to them for legal help or other advice.

2. *'Pass over to Calneh, and see, and from there go to Hamath the great; then go down to Gath of the Philistines. Are you better than these kingdoms? Or is their territory greater than your territory?'*

The background to this verse is probably the expansion of territory that was achieved during the reign of Jeroboam II (793–753 BC). No explanation is given in the text as to why Calneh, Hamath the Great, and Gath are specifically mentioned as examples for Israel. It could have been because they were prosperous cities, and yet they were no better off than Israel, since it was the recipient of the LORD's favour. More probably, they are cited as examples of opulent cities that had perished, and the warnings are there for Israel to heed. Calneh (Heb. *kalnêh*, though in Isa. 10:9, if it is the same city, it is spelt *kalnô*) was probably situated north of Aleppo, and it was the place that the Assyrians called Kullani. Hamath was on the Orontes river, about 200 km (125 miles) north of Damascus, though the territory it controlled must have extended further south as, according to 2 Kings 23:33 and 25:21, Riblah was within its borders. Gath was one of the five Philistine cities, and the only one of them not mentioned in the oracle against Gaza (1:6-8). It changed hands several times, and Uzziah broke down its wall (2 Chron. 26:6). The people of Israel are challenged to 'pass over to Calneh and see,' then to Hamath and finally to Gath. These great centres of civilisation were prime examples of major cities that had been destroyed and their glory dissipated. The questions at the end of the verse are intended to crystallise in the minds of the people of Israel the precariousness of its position: 'Are you better than these kingdoms? Or is their territory greater than your territory?' Both questions expect a negative response. Of course, Israel was no better (Heb. lit. 'good from,' *hatôvîm min-*) than them, and her territory, even though it had again reached the promised borders during the reigns of Jeroboam II and Uzziah, was still not of major size (2 Kings 14:23-29; 2 Chron. 26:6-15).

3. *'O you who put far away the day of disaster and bring near the seat of violence?'*

The characterisation of Israel following the 'woe' of verse 1 continues, as does the address in the second-person masculine plural. In describing the way in which the people have attempted to keep out of mind 'the day of disaster,' the verb used is rare (*nâdâh*, pi. part. masc. pl., *m^enaddîm*). It is a verb that only occurs twice in the Old Testament, here and in Isaiah 66:5. It means 'to thrust out,' and in post-Biblical Hebrew it was used to denote excommunication. What the people were doing was thrusting out of their minds the evil day. Nowhere else does the expression in the singular, 'evil day,' appear, though the plural, 'evil days,' is found in Psalm 49:5. The book of Amos contains several expressions involving the noun 'day,' including 'day of battle' (1:14), 'that day' (2:16), 'the day I punish Israel' (3:14), and 'the day of the LORD' (5:18, 20). 'Day' cannot be limited to a twenty-four hour period, and hence means a period of trouble or intense difficulty that lies ahead. The remainder of the verse has been translated in several different ways. The ESV rendering, 'bring near the seat of violence,' takes the Hebrew word *shévet* as a derivative from the verb 'to sit' or 'dwell,' *yâshav*. The NIV has a freer translation, 'and bring near a reign of terror,' presumably extending the idea of seat to embrace the thought of a regime of violence. More probably the word translated 'seat' in the ESV is derived from *shâvat*, 'to rest, come to an end,' and means 'a violent termination.'[1] This interpretation gives a good parallel in the verse. While refusing

[1] *DIHG-S*, p. 88, §71 (e).

to contemplate the true nature of the day of the LORD, by their sin and rebellion the people were bringing ever nearer the destruction of Samaria and the dissipation of the people.

4. *'Woe to those who lie on beds of ivory and stretch themselves out on their couches, and eat lambs from the flock and calves from the midst of the stall.'*

The description of a life of luxury and ease continues with reference to how the people reclined on beds and couches, thus demonstrating the opulence of the rich. Reference has already been made earlier to the use of ivory in houses (see comment on 3:15). The accusation against the people is that they: 'lie on beds of ivory.' The use of ivory was widespread in the Near East. Solomon imported it for his throne (1 Kings 10:18-20), while Sennacherib boasted about having taken, among other things, ivory beds from Hezekiah.[1] Presumably this relates to festive occasions in the houses, not to sacrificial feasts in the temple. The use of 'beds' points to domestic feasts, at which the rich would lounge on their 'couches.' The word for 'stretching themselves' (*sârach*) is used of curtains hanging free (Exod. 26:12; Ezek. 23:15), and so is applied here to the recumbent posture of those at the feasts. This is the first time in the Bible that reference is made to reclining at the table when eating, but it became standard practice much later (see Matt. 9:10; 26:7; Mark 14:18).[2] They feasted on 'lambs from the flock and calves from the midst of the stall.' This was not normal everyday fare, but meat from the animals that had been kept in the special feeding stalls. The stall (*marbêk*) was for fattening cattle, and the calf from the stall (*'êgel marbêk*) was the fatted calf (1 Sam. 28:24; Jer. 46:21).

[1] *ANET*, p. 288.

[2] The NT verb is *anakeimai*. See the entry in *A Greek-English Lexicon of the New Testament and Other Early Christian Literature*, 6th ed., revised and annotated by F. W. Danker (Chicago: University of Chicago Press, 2000), for further examples from 300 BC.

5. *'who sing idle songs to the sound of the harp and like David invent for themselves instruments of music.'*

Apart from feasting, these occasions were times of musical diversion. The memory of King David is recalled, not because of his leadership of the kingdom, but because of his musical prowess (see 1 Sam. 16:15-23). While the word for the harp (*nêvel*) is quite common, the verb associated with it (*pârat*) is not. The verb occurs nowhere else in the Old Testament, though a derived noun (*péret*) does appear in Leviticus 19:10 in relation to fallen grapes. 'Play' or 'improvise' certainly fit the context, though 'sing' is possible, especially as 'sound of the harps' is literally, 'on the mouth of the harp' (*'al pî hannâvel*). This last suggestion would imply that songs were sung to the accompaniment of the harp.[1] According to the Masoretic punctuation, the break should come after the word 'harp': 'they play on the harp; like David they improvise on instruments of music.' The verb translated 'invent' (*châshav*) really means 'to think' or 'consider,' and then 'to plan' or 'to invent.' The problem is how to understand it in relation to what the people were doing musically. No mention is ever made of David inventing musical instruments, though he did compose many songs (2 Sam. 23:1). The best solution seems to be to take the verb as meaning 'think themselves,' that is, the people in their carousing thought themselves to be like David the musician.[2] This was just another aspect of their pride.

6. *'who drink wine in bowls and anoint themselves with the finest oils, but are not grieved over the ruin of Joseph!'*

Other activities also marked out their behavioural patterns. The first of the further accusations is against people: 'who drink wine

[1] 'Sing' is one of three alternatives given in *DCH* for this verb. See VI, p. 765. For the interpretation, 'the words of the songs come forth as the music of the harp dictates,' see J. Niehaus, 'Amos,' p. 439.

[2] This is close to the translation of G. V. Smith, *Amos*, p. 195: 'They esteem themselves to be like David on instruments of music.'

in bowls.' The ESV's 'in bowls' represents the Hebrew word *mizrêq* that is only twice used of drinking bowls (here, and in Zech. 9:15). Usually, drinking bowls were used in connection with rituals of the ceremonial law, and they are included in the list of implements that were used at the altar (Num. 4:14). They were normally made of silver or gold, and could weigh as much as seventy shekels (Num. 7:85). The use of 'bowl,' instead of the more usual words for drinking vessels, points to the abuse of wine that was prevalent. The toiletries in use were also indicative of great wealth, for the accusation is that 'they anoint themselves with the finest oils.' Though the verb for anoint (*mâshach*) is often used of sacred anointing, here it is employed of rubbing oil on the body, just as it is used elsewhere of painting a house (Jer. 22:14), or putting oil on a shield (Isa. 21:5). 'Oils' (*sh^e^mânîm*) is a word that has many different meanings in the Old Testament. These range from oil that was used in the tabernacle/temple, to its use in cooking, or to oil that was traded as a commodity.

These material abuses are now replaced by one that went to the heart of Israelite religion. The accusation is: 'but are not grieved over the ruin of Joseph!' Joseph was another, and an appropriate name, for the northern kingdom (see its use already in 5:6). The occurrence of the word 'ruin' (*shêver*) to describe the coming desolation of Israel is important. This word, appearing forty-four times in the Old Testament, is employed twenty-eight times to depict the impending fall of Israel or Judah. Material things were so prominent in the life of Israel, that there was no thought for what was soon to happen. There was no sickness (Heb. *châlâh*, ni.) of heart concerning the impending collapse of the nation after two centuries of independent existence.[1]

[1] The variety of meanings are listed in *DCH*, VIII, pp. 448-49.

7. *'Therefore they shall now be the first of those who go into exile, and the revelry of those who stretch themselves out shall pass away.'*

Once more the word '*lâkên*,' 'therefore,' introduces a divine declaration concerning coming judgment (see the note on this word in the comments on 3:11). To it is added the word 'now' (*'attâh*). The significance of 'now' is that it marks the logical outcome, though not the temporal one.[1] Those addressed by this message would ironically keep their pre-eminent position, being the first to be led away into exile. The experience of exile was already threatened upon Gentiles (1:5). Now the message is that it will also be experienced by Israel. The attack upon Jerusalem by the Assyrians would finish the nation, for the LORD's assurance is that 'the revelry of those who stretch themselves out shall pass away.' 'Revelry' is clearly a general concept here, even though the word used for it elsewhere denotes funeral occasions (Jer. 16:5).

4. *Judgment against Pride (6:8-14)*

The section of Amos that conveys the messages to Israel (chaps. 3–6) concludes with a final condemnation of prevailing attitudes. It commences with a sworn announcement from the Sovereign God, and ends with the threat of invasion and exile. Those two things are interconnected, for it is the Lord of history who controls the destiny of nations, including Israel, and he uses other nations to carry out his purposes. Those who were showing pride in themselves will ultimately be humbled when God raises up Assyria to oppress them. This section comprises several short messages, all contributing to the overall theme.

[1] This point was made long ago by W. R. Harper, *Amos and Hosea*, p. 149: 'The *now* is logical, rather than temporal, Ho. 2^{10} 5^{7}.'

8. *The Lord GOD has sworn by himself, declares the LORD, the God of hosts: 'I abhor the pride of Jacob and hate his strongholds, and I will deliver up the city and all that is in it.'*

The section commences with the most solemn declaration possible, for it contains an oath: 'The Lord GOD has sworn by himself.' Divine oaths are part of the warp and weft of the Old Testament. They stand at the forefront of the covenantal relationship between God and his people. While people swore by the deity, God did not need to do so, swearing by himself, with this aspect being emphasised (see this placed at the forefront at Heb. 6:16-18).[1] This form of expression denotes the definitive and final nature of God's declaration. The title given to God (*yhwh 'elôhê hatsts^e vâ'ôt*) has already been used in 4:13, with a similar one in 3:13 (*'adônay 'elôhê hatsts^e vâ'ôt*). The first part of the declaration concerns the understanding the people of Israel had of themselves: The LORD says: 'I abhor the pride of Jacob and hate his strongholds.' His attitude is expressed using a verb that only occurs here in the Old Testament (*metâ'êv*, pi. part. of *tâ'av*), though it may be a by-form of another verb for 'abhor' that occurs on many more occasions (*tâ'av*). The meaning is quite clear in the context, however, as the parallel verb in the next colon is 'to hate' (*sânê'*).[2] What the Almighty hated was 'the pride of Jacob.' While in Psalm 47:4 'the pride of Jacob' is what God loves, and is clearly the land of Canaan, here the expression relates rather to the attitude of the people. Nowhere in the Old Testament does

[1] The verbal form here (*nishba'*) is a *nif'al* that has as the subject the one doing the action and at the same time the one on whom the action is done. This double-duty use of the *nif'al* serves as a reflexive form. See, *IBHS*, pp. 387-88, §23.4. Hebrew possesses no reflexive pronouns. Two verbal forms, *nif'al* and especially *hitpa'el*, are used to express reflexive action. In addition, as here with the use of *b^e nafshô*, 'by himself,' suffixed personal pronouns also serve to fill the lack. See, Ronald J. Williams, *Hebrew Syntax: An Outline*, 2nd ed. (Toronto: University of Toronto Press, 1984), p. 25, §130.

[2] The LXX recognised this by translating the first verb by *bdelussomai* ('to abhor'), and the second one by *miseô* ('to hate').

God express hatred of the land of his choice. The self-elevation of the people in their own eyes was what he despised. He also hated their fortresses, as by choosing the capital as Samaria and building a fortified city, the people thought themselves to be impregnable. The judgments already passed on Samaria (see 2:13-16; 3:6, 11-15; 4:2, 3; 5:3-10, 16, 17, 25-27; 6:7) are confirmed in the most solemn way, though it is not only Samaria that will experience God's judgment. The word for city here (*'îr*) does not have the article with it, *the* city, which would be expected if Samaria was the only city in view. It is, therefore, better to take it as a reference to 'each and every city.'[1] Whatever was contained in a city—its people, its defensive equipment, its stores—was going to be delivered over to the invading Assyrians, who were notorious for their pillaging (Isa. 10:13, 14).

9-11. *And if ten men remain in one house, they shall die. And when one's relative, the one who anoints him for burial, shall take him up to bring the bones out of the house, and shall say to him who is in the innermost parts of the house, 'Is there still anyone with you?' he shall say, 'No'; and he shall say, 'Silence! We must not mention the name of the* L*ORD.'*

9, 10. The consequences of God's judgment against Israel are now depicted by a hypothetical scene. The question at hand is: what will it be like when God's judgment visits us? The answer is given here. Presumably it is a large house, a mansion, which is in view, perhaps with a large extended family living in it. Ten men in it die. Then one of the family, a *dôd*, comes to bury the dead. This word often designates a paternal uncle, but at times it is used more widely of someone's relative by kinship or marriage, and this fits the picture here. The Hebrew text can be translated, 'and if a relative, and the one who is to burn the bodies, carries them out of the house,' which would mean that two people were coming

[1] J. Niehaus, 'Amos,' p. 443, has an excellent note regarding this.

into the house. However, the NIV translation ('And if a relative who is to burn the bodies comes to carry them out of the house'), which identifies the one burning the bodies as the relative, is also possible.[1] Cremation was not a normal practice in Israel, except for some serious sins (see Lev. 20:14; 21:9). Achan's body was burnt (Josh. 7:15, 25), as were the bodies of Saul and Jonathan (1 Sam. 31:12). Perhaps the picture is of so many dead people in the house that burning was the only feasible way to dispose of the bodies. A survivor is in the house, and when asked, 'Is there still anyone with you?', he will say: 'No.' This is not the usual negative, but a noun meaning 'end' or 'limit' (*'êfes*). It can, however, be used in the sense of 'there is not, there is no one,' and this fits the context here.[2] 'And he shall say, "Silence! We must not mention the name of the Lord."'[3] Two questions immediately arise as to the meaning of this. First, the word 'Silence' (Heb. *hâs*) is used elsewhere to quieten people, such as prior to the reading of the law (Neh. 8:11), or before the presence of the LORD (Hab. 2:20; Zeph. 1:7; Zech. 2:13). Here it is used calling for silence in the face of the impending disaster that is facing the nation. Secondly, the reason for not mentioning the LORD's name is unexplained. The best understanding is to say that calling upon God would be inappropriate in the circumstances. Covenantal punishment is to be meted out, and no attempt should be made to alleviate it. The LORD's visitation in judgment must be allowed to take its course.

[1] The NIV translation assumes that 'and his burner' (*ûm^{e}sârefô*) is epexegetical of the preceding phrase, 'and the one lifting him up' (*ûn^{e}sâ'ô*). Normally the epexegetical word would not be preceded by the conjunction. However, the following verb ('and he will say,' *v^e'âmar*) is singular. Another anomaly is that the verb 'to burn' is spelt with *samek*, not the usual *shin*.

[2] For other examples, see the listing in *DCH*, I, p. 359.

[3] The lit. rendering of this sentence is 'for not to mention the name of the LORD' (*kî lo' l^{e}hazkîr b^{e}shem yhwh*). The ESV translation is good, for the inf. constr. *hazkîr* is used like a verbal noun. See Ronald J. Williams, *Hebrew Syntax*, p. 36, §196, and p. 66, §397.

11. The explanation now follows as to why the events already described are going to take place: 'For behold, the LORD commands.' The first word, 'for' (*kî*), need not be stressed to mean strictly that what follows is a statement of the reason for God's dealings with Samaria and Israel. Rather, it serves here as a particle linking verses 8-10 with what follows. The form of expression is indicative of a prophetic announcement of God's intentions, especially those concerning judgment (see 4:2: 'behold, the days are coming upon you …,' and 6:14: 'For behold, I will raise up against you a nation …'). It gives special solemnity to the words: 'Behold, the LORD …' This is followed by the word 'commanding' (*m^etsavveh*, pi. part. masc. s.), a participial form that appears in covenantal contexts in which God is enforcing his demands on the people. It is used in passages such as Exodus 34:11, Deuteronomy 26:16, and Jeremiah 34:22. The declaration is to the effect that the LORD will smite both large and small houses so that they are broken into pieces. The meaning of the words 'fragments' (*r^esîsîm*) and 'bits' (*b^eqi'îm*) is quite clear from the context even though both are rare, the former only occurring here while the latter appears elsewhere only in Isaiah 22:9. The verb 'struck down' (*nâkâh*, hi.), while often occurring in the general sense of 'hit,' is specifically used of God's action in striking in punishment.[1]

12, 13. *Do horses run on rocks? Does one plough there with oxen? But you have turned justice into poison and the fruit of righteousness into wormwood—you who rejoice in Lo-debar, who say, 'Have we not by our own strength captured Karnaim for ourselves?'*

12. In the ESV translation there are two questions in this verse, the first requiring a negative answer, while the second expects a positive answer. The first question poses what is ridiculous. Who

[1] See the entries in *DCH*, V, p. 685.

would try and race horses over rocks? The reader expects the second question to require a negative answer, but its form in the ESV needs a positive one—of course oxen are used in ploughing. Two possible solutions can be advanced. The first is to argue that the word 'rocks' does double duty, and hence it has to be understood as the indirect accusative in the second question: 'Does one plough [the rocky crags] with oxen?' The same effect can be achieved by rendering like the NJKV, NIV and ESV: 'Does one plough *there* with oxen?' The alternative is to propose a wrong division of words in the MT, assuming that the plural ending of oxen (*-îm*) has been mistaken for the Hebrew word for sea (*yâm*): 'Does one plough the sea with oxen?' (NRSV). This proposal involves a redivision of words and changed vocalisation. Also, it removes an oddity in that the word for oxen is a masculine plural form (*beqârîm*), though in the singular (*bâqâr*) it is a collective noun, and hence the verb does not need to be plural. The harder reading is to retain the MT text, and accept the double duty function of 'rocky crags.'

These questions lead on to the further assertion: 'But you have turned justice into poison and the fruit of righteousness into wormwood.' This assertion is connected with the questions in this way. The foolishness of trying to run horses or plough oxen on rocks was blatantly obvious. Similarly it should have been evident that violation of the moral order would bring consequences for society and ultimately it would result in God's judgment on the people. There is an echo here of what was said already at 5:7, but with two precise parallels—justice/fruit of righteousness and poison/wormwood. 'Justice' (*mishpât*) and 'righteousness' (*tsedâqâh*) were paired in 5:7 whereas here 'fruit of righteousness' (*perî tsedâqâh*) is used without any great difference in meaning. 'Fruit' is a metaphorical expression to denote an outcome, and while used positively (see Prov. 11:30, 'the fruit of the righteous is a tree of life') it is also employed elsewhere in negative expressions (see Hos. 10:13, 'fruit of lies'). 'Fruit of righteousness' also became a New Testament expression (see Phil. 1:11; James 3:18). 'Poison' (*r'osh*) and 'wormwood' (*la'anâh*) were both bitter plants, and they form a fixed pair in the Old Testament.[1] Once more the perversion of justice in Israel is brought under divine scrutiny and condemnation.

13. Another claim of the people is set aside by Amos' message. Territorial expansion had taken place under Jeroboam II, who 'restored the boundaries of Israel from Lebo Hamath to the Sea of the Arabah' (2 Kings 14:25). This created in the minds of the people the idea that their military strength would provide defence against foreign aggression. That view is now challenged by Amos: 'you who rejoice in Lo-debar who say, "Have we not by our own strength captured Karnaim for ourselves?"' Here a play on words takes place, something that Amos does elsewhere as well (see the play on 'summer fruits' and 'end' in 8:1, 2). Lo-debar was about 16 km (10 miles) south-east of the Sea of Kinnereth (Galilee), while Karnaim was to the east of it in Bashan. Lo-debar is mentioned in 2 Samuel 9:4 and 17:27, with a slight variation in spelling between the two passages (*lô dever* in the first, and *lo' dever* in the second). However, here Amos calls it *lo' dâvâr*, which means 'a thing of nought, nothing.' *Karnaim* is the Hebrew word for 'horns,' the symbol of a bull's strength, and metaphorically used to denote 'power' or 'might.' The claim the people were making was that they, by their might, had achieved the victory over Karnaim. The prophet is implying 'you by bullish strength have captured nothing.'[2] The claim they were making was that without divine intervention they had managed to obtain Lo-debar and Karnaim 'for themselves' (*lânû*). This should be retained in translation (as

[1] For the listings, see *DCH*, IV, p. 556.

[2] This is the translation of P. C. Craigie, *Twelve Prophets*, vol. 1 (*Daily Study Bible*: Edinburgh: Saint Andrew Press, 1984), p. 172. Craigie goes on to say: 'If, in a later age, Robin Hood and his men captured Nottingham, Amos would have called it "Nothingham."'

in the RSV, NASB, NKJV, NRSV and ESV), as it emphasises not just victory but acquisition of territory.[1]

> 14. *'For behold, I will raise up against you a nation, O house of Israel,' declares the* Lord, *the God of hosts; 'and they shall oppress you from Lebo-hamath to the Brook of the Arabah.'*

A solemn declaration by the Lord concludes the oracles against Israel. It commences similarly to verse 11, and the Hebrew word order should be preserved, as it focuses attention straight away on the action that is going to affect Israel: 'For behold, I will raise up against you a nation …' To 'rise up against' (*qûm 'al*) is a common Old Testament way of describing hostile action against someone. The opponent is simply noted as 'a nation' (*gôy*) without any further specification, though clearly it is Assyria that is in view (see 5:27). It was going to 'oppress' (*lâchats*) them, probably an allusion to the treatment that Israel received in Egypt long before (Exod. 22:21, 22; 23:9). This judgment that was going to overtake Israel would extend from 'Lebo hamath to the Brook of the Arabah.' 'Lebo' could be 'entrance' (lit. 'from where one goes into Hamath'), as this was almost a standard expression to denote the northern frontier of Israel (see Num. 13:21; 34:8; Josh. 13:5; Judg. 3:3; 1 Kings 8:65). The southern frontier was the brook of Arabah. No name is given to this brook, but it was probably on the northern end of the Dead Sea, so marking out the boundary between Israel and Judah. The Dead Sea was sometimes referred to as 'the Sea of the Arabah' (Deut. 3:17; Josh. 3:16; 2 Kings 14:25). The solemnity of this judgment message is highlighted by the use of the title for God of 'the Lord God Almighty,' and the designation

[1] The one version that is different from all others is the *NEB*: 'Jubilant over nothing, you boast, "Have we not won power by our own strength?"' This denies that Lo Debar and Karnaim were meant as place names. However, the book is replete with geographical references and hence it is better to retain the names while recognising that there is word play here.

of the message as a divine declaration (*ne'um*; for its meaning and use see the comments on 2:11).

Application

Human pride has been evident right from the entrance of sin (Gen. 3:6, 7). Like those building the tower of Babel, many others in Old Testament history sought to make a name for themselves (Gen. 11:4). In this passage, Amos' message relates to pride in human achievement. In Israel, fortresses were built (verse 8), and military victories lauded (verse 13). Amos' contemporaries, Isaiah and Hosea, had to bring similar accusations against Israel (Isa. 25:11; Hos. 5:5; 7:10). The people did not realise that God was going to humble the nation by bringing the Assyrians to devastate the land (verses 8, 14). The New Testament continues to warn against pride, and of our need to humble ourselves under the mighty hand of God (1 Pet. 5:5, 6; James 4:6). That attitude is not natural for us, and hence we have to ask for a spirit of humility to be given to us so we can willingly respond in love and faith to God's demands on us.

5

Visions of Judgment (7:1–9:10)

The conclusion of chapter 6 completes the earlier part of the prophecy of Amos in setting out the oracles against the nations surrounding Israel (1:3–2:5), and then concentrating the focus on Israel (2:6–6:14). Now, in the second major part of the prophecy, a series of visions is presented. Several factors call for general comment before the individual sections are discussed.

1. One of the modes of communication to the prophets was by vision. Two Hebrew verbs (*râ'âh* and *châzâh*) are used in this connection, and they seem to be practically synonymous (for *râ'âh*, see Isa. 6:1; Jer. 1:11; Ezek. 1:1; and for *châzâh*, see Amos 1:1; Ezek. 13:8). 'Seeing' in this sense was more than just observing something with the eye. It was one of the means that God used at times to reveal himself to his messengers.

2. The series of visions differs from the earlier oracles in that they do not concentrate on the social, moral, and religious sins of Israel. Rather, they pay attention to the preaching ministry of Amos, something on which the earlier chapters are silent.

3. Visions 3, 4, and 5 all have appendices. The one attached to the third vision is the account of interaction between Amos and Amaziah, the priest at Bethel. This is important because of the biographical information concerning Amos that it gives, and

about his call to serve as a prophet. The fourth vision is followed by oracles declaring the coming judgment, and this is couched in terms of 'the day of the LORD,' though that precise expression is not used. Instead, 'in that day' occurs twice (8:9, 13) and 'the days are coming' once (8:11). The fifth and final vision is followed by declarations concerning God's lordship, and then eschatological presentations again using the terms 'in that day' (9:11) and 'the days are coming' (9:13). This final section also includes the most direct elements of hope in the prophecy. The promise is given of the restoration of David's tent (9:11, 12; see Acts 15:15-18) and of return from exile (9:13-15).

4. The five visions have a distinct literary genre, forming two pairs and one single vision. The pattern is as follows:[1]

a. Visions 1 and 2 (7:1-3 and 7:4-6)		
1. Introductory formula	7:1a	7:4a
2. Optical content	7:1	7:4
3. Prophet's intercession	7:2	7:5
4. The LORD's response	7:3	7:6
b. Visions 3 and 4 (7:7-9 and 8:1-3)		
1. Introductory formula	7:7	8:1
2. Optical content	7:7	8:1
3. Dialogue	7:8	8:2
4. Interpretation	7:8	8:2
5. Concluding judgment	7:9	8:3
+ appendices	7:10-17	8:4-8
c. Vision 5 (9:1-15)		
1. Introductory formula	9:1a	
2. The LORD's command	9:1b-c	
3. The LORD's judgement	9:1d-4a	
4. Concluding verdict	9:4b	
+appendices	9:5-15	

[1] This outline is following the very helpful discussion by C. Hassell Bullock, *An Introduction to the Old Testament Prophetic Books* (Chicago: Moody Press, 1986), p. 71. For another outline, see Douglas Stuart, *Hosea-Jonah*, p. 368, that is followed by J. Niehaus, 'Amos,' p. 450.

5. No information is supplied regarding how these visions were recorded by Amos, or whether he used them in his public ministry. What is clear, however, is that they mark a move forward by the prophet in regard to the challenges facing Israel, for there is progression of thought regarding the coming of the LORD in judgment on the land.

1. *The First Vision—A Plague of Locusts (7:1-3)*

> 1. *This is what the Lord GOD showed me: behold, he was forming locusts when the latter growth was just beginning to sprout, and behold, it was the latter growth after the king's mowings.*

No indication is given whether these visions were contemporaneous with the oracles that were given in the earlier part of the prophecy, or if they were revealed at some other time. The introductory word, 'This [is] ...' (Heb. *koh*) is not looking backward to what has preceded, but forward to what follows. It is probably an abbreviation of the fuller formula, 'Thus says the LORD' (see comment on 1:3), and it quite frequently introduces judgmental messages. Amos is shown (lit. 'he caused me to see,' *hir'anî*) the preparation of swarms of locusts. A verb (*yôtsêr*, part. masc. s.) is used to describe the creative work of God. It has already been used in 4:13 regarding his forming the mountains. It is, along with 'create' (*bârâ'*) and 'make' (*'âsâh*), often used of God's creation of the universe (Isa. 45:18), the earth (Jer. 33:2), and, as here, of natural phenomena (see also Psa. 74:17 and 95:5). The word for 'locusts' (*govay*) only occurs here and in Nahum 3:17, and apparently is a collective term for locusts. The context requires some insect that feeds on plants, and the LXX understood it as locusts (*epigone akridôn*, 'offspring of locusts').[1] The timing of this plague is said to be 'king's

[1] Apparently the LXX translators took the word *yôtsêr* as *yêtser*, in the sense of 'offspring,' though its normal meaning is 'thinking,' 'imagination.'

mowings.' Nowhere else is this mentioned, but seemingly the king had the right to the first mowing of crops. This was probably a form of taxation to support the bureaucracy of the kingdom. The word for 'second crop' (*léqesh*) is a *hapax legomenon*, but it is known from outside the Bible in the Geza calendar that dates from the 10th century BC. It refers to the new grass and herbs that spring up as a result of the late rains in March and April.[1] The threat conveyed by this picture was that the people would be deprived of the food crops they needed to carry them through till the next harvest.

2. *When they had finished eating the grass of the land, I said, 'O Lord GOD, please forgive! How can Jacob stand? He is so small!'*

The prophet saw the result of the plague. When the locusts had completely eaten (Heb. lit. 'it [the swarm] completed to eat') the grass of the land, the prophet cries out, 'O Lord GOD, please forgive! How can Jacob stand? He is so small!' The appeal is for forgiveness, as the prophet sensed that the picture he had been given was of judgment from the LORD on Israel. He asks for God's mercy to be shown to an erring people, though he makes no appeal to the covenantal relationship. The following question starts in Hebrew with the interrogative marker, 'Who?' (*mî*). This is one of the examples in the Old Testament often cited of this word being used in the sense normally expressed by *mâh*, 'how,' 'what.'[2] The verb here is 'to stand' (*yâqûm*), which has the idea of standing one's ground, like its usage in Psalm 24:3: 'Who shall ascend the hill of the LORD? And who shall stand (*yâqûm*) in his holy place?' Alternately, *mî* can be given its usual meaning, 'Who?', and the rendering will be, 'Who is Jacob that he can stand?'[3] This translation fits well, and the reason

[1] See J. C. L. Gibson, *Textbook of Syrian Semitic Inscriptions, vol. 1 Hebrew and Moabite Inscriptions*, pp. 1-4.

[2] See *DIHG~S*, p. 8, §8, *Rem.* 2.

[3] This is the suggestion in *IBHS*, p. 320, §18.e.

given in response to the question for this is that Jacob is so small. This is puzzling at first sight, because Jacob/Israel was much larger and wealthier than the southern kingdom of Judah. However, the comparison is probably not between Israel and Judah, but between Israel and the LORD: in comparison with the power of God, Israel seemed so small and frail.

> 3. *The* LORD *relented concerning this: 'It shall not be,' said the* LORD.

God's attitude to the prophet's response was to defer any judgment. The word translated by the ESV as 'relented' (*nâcham*, pi.) is used quite frequently of God. On various occasions he 'relented' or 'repented,' in regard to actions he was going to take after appropriate responses to his words (for other examples, see 1 Chron. 21:15; Jer. 18:8; 26:3, 19; Jon. 3:10). The declaration made by God was: 'It shall not be' (lit. *lo' tihyeh*). This was a way of expressing the certainty that something would not come to pass. Identical words were used in connection with the threatened invasion of Judah from Syria and Israel during Isaiah's ministry: 'it shall not come to pass' (*lo' tihyeh*, Isa. 7:7).

2. *The Second Vision—Fire (7:4-6)*

> 4. *This is what the Lord* GOD *showed me: behold, the Lord* GOD *was calling for a judgment by fire, and it devoured the great deep and was eating up the land.*

Identical introductory words occur in 7:1. The prophet now sees God calling for judgment by fire. One of the symbolical meanings of the Hebrew word for 'fire' (*'êsh*) is judgment. Fire cuts off access to the tree of life (Gen. 3:24), while Sodom and Gomorrah were destroyed by fire (Gen. 19:24). The use of the participle, 'was calling' (*qôrê'*), indicates progressive activity, namely that God was in the process of calling for judgment to come on Israel.[1] The judgment, when it came, resulted in the drying up of 'the great deep' (*tᵉhôm*). This is the word used in Genesis 1:2 of the primeval deep, but it also holds other connotations. For example, it occurs in Genesis 7:11 of the ocean, while in Isaiah 51:10 it refers to the Red Sea when Israel crossed it. Here it seems to be a general reference to an ocean that is devoured by fire (Hebrew uses the verb, *'âkal*, 'to eat,' to describe the fire's effect). The fire also consumed the land (Heb. *chêleq*, 'a portion'), a natural opposite to ocean. The use of this particular word to describe the land of Canaan, or part of it, may have been chosen deliberately, since the verb from which it came (*châlaq*) is used in the biblical text regarding the apportionment of Canaan to Israel (see Josh. 18:5). The threat is all the more serious since it is against the territory that had been given by the LORD for his people.

5. *Then I said, 'O Lord GOD, please cease! How can Jacob stand? He is so small!'*

He speaks, attempting to get God to desist from further judgment: 'please cease! ' Then follows the same question and answer that appeared in the preceding section: 'How can Jacob stand? He is so small!' As with the previous section (see verse 2, and the commentary), it is best to render this, 'Who is Jacob that he should stand?' The answer again draws attention to how small Jacob is in comparison to God's might.

6. *The LORD relented concerning this: 'This also shall not be,' said the Lord GOD.*

The answer is also a repetition of verse 3, with two slight alterations. One is the addition of the word 'also' (*gam*) or 'either,' that

[1] Usually the Hebrew *qôrê' bᵉ* means 'to call upon,' 'to pray to,' but here it indicates 'calling for' fire to come upon Israel as an exhibition of God's righteous anger with the people.

simply indicates this verse's connection with the preceding section. The other is the alteration of the name of God from 'LORD' (*yhwh*) to 'Lord GOD' (*'adonây yhwh*). This is part of the variation of divine names throughout this book.

3. *The Third Vision—The Wall (7:7-9)*

> 7. *This is what he showed me: behold, the Lord was standing beside a wall built with a plumb line, with a plumb line in his hand.*

The report of the third vision commences in a similar way to the previous ones, though the formula is abbreviated slightly: 'Thus he showed me, and behold ...' The change may occur because the subject that follows is 'the Lord.' What he saw was 'the Lord was standing beside a wall built with a plumb line.' The implication is that the Lord had taken his stance there (the verb is *nâtsav*, ni.), not just that he happened to stand by the wall. It probably has military overtones, as the Assyrian equivalent (*izuzzum*) is used in accounts of enemy troops taking their stand for battle. The expression describes him as being 'beside the wall of the plumb' (*'al chômat 'anâk*). Several problems of translation and interpretation emerge at this point. The word translated 'plumb' only occurs here and in the following verse. The traditional view has been that it means 'lead,' and hence the lead weight that was placed on the plumb line to check the walls of buildings. One difficulty with this view is that *'anâk* appears to be a loan word from the Assyrian *anâku* that means 'tin,' or some other metal. Another difficulty is that the expression is 'by a wall of ...' suggesting that what follows is comparable to 'a fortified wall of bronze' (Jer. 15:20), or 'an iron wall' (Ezek. 4:3). A third difficulty is that Hebrew already had a technical word for plumb line (*mishqelet*, 2 Kings 21:13; Isa. 28:17). A fourth is the pattern in the two previous visions, which suggests the same pattern will carry over here. In those earlier visions what was seen was the instrument of judgment (locusts, fire). Hence, here in verses 7, 8, the word *'ᵃnâk* should represent a tool or instrument of judgment. A plumb line did not take on that characteristic. Attempts have been made to defend the traditional view, but the Hebrew has to be paraphrased to mean 'a wall built with a plumb line.'[1] What is known is that in various Near Eastern documents reference is made to metal walls with military connotations,[2] and the LXX rendering (*epi teichous adamantinou*, 'upon a wall of adamant') supports this. The LXX is the earliest translation of the Hebrew Old Testament and some credence should be given to it. The Greek word *adamas* means 'steel' (alternately, 'diamond'). If this view is correct, then the metal wall denotes Assyria, which was going to come with all its might against Israel.[3] The traditional view, however, is defended by various modern commentators.[4]

> 8. *And the* Lord *said to me, 'Amos, what do you see?' And I said, 'A plumb line.' Then the Lord said, 'Behold, I am setting a plumb line in the midst of my people Israel; I will never again pass by them.'*

A question is now addressed to the prophet by the Lord, with no indication that he is open to intercession on behalf of the people by the prophet: 'Amos, what do you see?' This is a regular procedure in prophetic visionary experiences (see Zech. 4:2; 5:2). Amos responds that he sees steel, to which the Lord says: 'Behold,[5] I am setting steel

[1] For a defence of that point of view, see J. A. Motyer, *The Day of the Lion*, pp. 161-62.

[2] For illustrations, see J. Niehaus, 'Amos,' p. 456.

[3] This is the interpretation followed by J. Niehaus, *ibid.*, and by Douglas Stuart, *Hosea-Jonah*, p. 373.

[4] See, e.g., T. E. McComiskey, 'Amos,' p. 321; Billy K. Smith, 'Amos,' p. 132; D. A. Hubbard, *Joel and Amos* (Tyndale Old Testament Commentaries: Leicester: Inter-Varsity Press, 1989), pp. 209-10.

[5] The form is the particle *hinnêh*, 'behold,' plus the 1 s. suffix, 'behold, I ...'

in the midst of (*b^eqérev*) my people Israel.' The insertion of 'behold' attracts attention to what follows. The LORD says: 'I will never again pass by them.' The literal translation of the Hebrew is, 'I will not again cross over to him.' This appears to mean, 'I will no longer pass over his transgression,' with the full expression occurring in Micah 7:18 (*v^e'ovêr 'al pésha'*). The threat is that divine mercy will no longer be extended to Israel, and the wrath of Assyrian military might will be unleashed against her. This is the first time in the prophecy that the LORD calls Israel 'my people' (for further instances, see verse 15; 8:2; 9:10, 14). This is comparable with Isaiah's usage, as the 8th-century prophets did not regard the sin of Israel and the coming punishment at the hands of Assyria as destroying the covenantal bond.

9. *'the high places of Isaac shall be made desolate, and the sanctuaries of Israel shall be laid waste, and I will rise against the house of Jeroboam with the sword.'*

The coming invasion by the Assyrians will mean the destruction of the special places of worship (see the comment on 4:13). During the history of Israel there were clearly a multiplicity of worship centres (see Elijah's references to the breaking down of the LORD's altars, 1 Kings 19:10, 14). The first two colons form exact parallelism. The use of Isaac/Israel (Jacob's father) is unusual but understandable (see its use again in verse 16), and the combination be made desolate/laid waste describes the result of devastation by an invading army. The annihilation of the ruling line of Jeroboam is threatened by announcing that the LORD will rise against it (Heb. *qûm 'al*) with the sword. The LORD could and did use the sword of invading armies to bring destruction on Israel. In the earlier prophecies in chapters 2-6, all the judgments were directed against the leaders in Israel, but here one man, the king, is singled out for judgment.

Application

God did not act against his people without forewarning issued by his prophets. He announced his plan to them (3:7). Here Amos presents three visions of judgment. After the first two, the Lord showed mercy and declared that the judgment would not happen (verses 3 and 6). This does not occur with the third vision. God is indeed 'merciful and gracious, slow to anger and abounding in steadfast love and faithfulness' (Psa. 86:15). He is patient, 'not wishing that any should perish, but that all should reach repentance' (2 Pet. 3:9). However, as Amos shows here, we cannot trifle with God's declarations, but must heed his word, repent, turn to him, and prove our repentance through our actions (Acts 26:20).

4. *Interaction between Prophet, Priest and King (7:10-17)*

10. *Then Amaziah the priest of Bethel sent to Jeroboam king of Israel, saying, 'Amos has conspired against you in the midst of the house of Israel. The land is not able to bear all his words.'*

A break in the sequence of visions occurs with the insertion of a historical incident. Amaziah was the resident priest at the Bethel shrine, who probably also had a particularly close relationship with Jeroboam II, king of Israel (793–753 BC). He sent a message to the king, either by letter or by a messenger, concerning the work of Amos. It began: 'Amos has conspired against you in the midst of the house of Israel.' Kings, especially among the northern tribes that formed Israel, were very susceptible to conspiracies against them. This was because no hereditary line of kings existed, as compared with the Davidic dynasty in Judah. Many kings were killed by relatives or rivals. The accusation was that Amos was trying to promote a conspiracy 'in the midst of the house of Israel' (*b^e^qérev bêt yisrâ'ēl*).

The expression is unusual, in that a reference to a conspiracy in the midst of the land, or something similar, is what is expected. Could it be that Amaziah was implying that Amos was conspiring with some in the royal household? Amaziah personalises the land in declaring that it cannot bear with all his words.

11. *For thus Amos has said, 'Jeroboam shall die by the sword, and Israel must go into exile away from his land.'*

The first comment on this verse must be concerning its reference to the *spoken* ministry of Amos. He was one of the first group of writing prophets in the 8th century BC (Hosea, Micah, Amos and Isaiah), as distinct from the earlier preaching prophets like Elijah and Elisha. However, it is clear that there never was a sharp separation between their public ministry by speech and their written messages. Amos' message is summarised as being devoted to the question of how Jeroboam would die and the coming devastation by the Assyrians that would result in exile for most of Israel. If he had not heard of the content of Amos' preaching, he now had this report to alert him to the threats, not only to the nation, but also to himself. The immediately preceding context speaks of the threat of the sword being visited upon the house of Jeroboam (verse 9) without any sure indication that Amos' preaching had reached Jeroboam himself. The certainty of exile, 'Israel must go into exile' (*v[e]yisrâ'ēl gâloh yigleh*), is expressed in the same way as the doom of Gilgal in 5:5 (*gâloh yigleh*), with the added description that it would be 'away from his land.' This phrase (*mê'al 'admâtô*, lit. 'from his land') simply reinforces the concept. It was not just servanthood within the land about which Amos was prophesying, but exile in a foreign country. Exactly the same description is used in 7:17, but with the additional note that the location of exile will be in an impure country (*'[a]dâmâh t[e]mê'âh*).

12. *And Amaziah said to Amos, 'O seer, go, flee away to the land of Judah, and eat bread there, and prophesy there.'*

Amaziah's message was blunt in the extreme. 'O seer, go.' According to the priest at Bethel there was no place for Amos in Israel. His marching orders were to 'go.' He called him a 'seer' (*chozeh*), an earlier word for prophet (see 1 Sam. 9:9). The word derived from the fact that revelation from God was often communicated in visionary form, and the verb from which 'seer' comes (*châzâh*) is one of the common verbs for 'seeing' in this sense (see Amos 1:1; Mic. 1:1; Isa. 1:1). The message to Amos continued: 'flee away to the land of Judah and eat bread there, and prophesy there.' The MT uses the verb 'to flee' (*bârach*) which suggests Amaziah was indicating that haste was needed on Amos' part. If he did not flee, then Jeroboam would seek his life. He had to go back home, 'to the land of Judah,' from where he had come (see 1:1, 'among the shepherds of Tekoa'). It was there, in Judah, that he would earn his living. 'Eat bread there': not a great deal of evidence is given in the Old Testament regarding the provision of sustenance for the prophets. Elijah was fed supernaturally when he was hiding in the ravine of Kerith (1 Kings 17:2-6), while Obadiah, the supervisor of Ahab's palace, hid a hundred prophets to save them from the pogrom that Jezebel had instituted, and provided them with food and water (1 Kings 18:2-4). Here Amaziah is implying that Amos' sustenance would be provided back home in Judah, for there he could 'eat bread' and also carry on with his prophetic ministry. '*There* prophesy' is emphatic in Hebrew (*shâm tinnâvê'*), marking the contrast between Amos' actions in the north and what he would continue to do when he returned home to Judah. Prophecies such as those he was uttering were unacceptable to king and priest in Israel, but may well have been pleasant to the ears of the people in Judah.

13. *'but never again prophesy at Bethel, for it is the king's sanctuary, and it is a temple of the kingdom.'*

Any further prophesying at Bethel was forbidden. The objection was made on the basis that Amos was operating a prophetic ministry right in the heart of the kingdom. 'The king's sanctuary' and 'the temple of the kingdom' appear to be two different expressions that describe the one location. The term for 'sanctuary' (*miqdâsh*) is used elsewhere of both the tabernacle and the temple, while 'house' (*báyit*) could be used of the temple (see its use in regard to David's desire to build the 'house' for the LORD in Jerusalem, 2 Sam. 7:5). When the nation divided after Solomon's death, Bethel was the most important cultic centre in the south of Israel (and nearest to Jerusalem), and sacrifices were offered there (1 Kings 12:31-33). It remained an important centre for Israel and 'the temple of the kingdom' remained located there.

14. *Then Amos answered and said to Amaziah, 'I was no prophet, nor a prophet's son, but I was a herdsman and a dresser of sycamore figs.'*

This answer by Amos has occasioned much discussion. On the face of it, he was insisting that he had only been a shepherd, being neither a prophet nor part of a prophetic group. His claim was that by employment he was 'a herdsman' (*bôqêr*) who looked after cattle (*bâqâr*), though in the next verse Amos indicates that he also cared for 'the flock' (*hatstso'n*), a word that could signify care for both sheep and goats. He was also 'a dresser of sycamore figs.' The word rendered 'dresser' (*bôlês*) only occurs here in the Old Testament, though its connection with 'sycamore fig trees' (*shiqmîm*) makes its translation relatively easy. The first sentence is a nominal one in Hebrew, having no verb. It is simply 'Not a prophet I,' but in English inclusion of a verb is necessary. The question in debate is: should the verb here be present tense, ('I *am* not a prophet'), or past tense ('I *was* not a prophet')? The context seems to support the past tense for two reasons: first, the use of the present tense contradicts the fact that Amos is a prophet, and, secondly, it suits the context better because the contrast is between his present role as a prophet and what he was previously. Amos is denying that he grew up being a member of the professional class of prophets, and that he came into the role of prophet through his membership of a collective band of prophets. His call was instead directly from God, so that a farmer became a prophet.[1]

15. *But the* Lord *took me from following the flock, and the* Lord *said to me, 'Go, prophesy to my people Israel.'*

Amos recounts his initial call from the Lord. He was taken from his role as a shepherd (*mê'ach*ᵃ*rê hatstso'n*, lit. 'from behind the flock') in order to become a prophet. His ministry was specifically to the northern kingdom: 'Go, prophesy to my people Israel.' Amos' recollection of his call is in marked contrast to what Amaziah had just said to him; merely 'Go … to the land of Judah … and there prophesy' (verse 12, *lêk … el 'erets y*ᵉ*hûdâh … shâm tinnâvê'*). This stood in direct opposition to the divine command: 'Go, prophesy to my people Israel' (*lêk hinnâvê' 'el 'ammî yisrâ'êl*). The Lord's direction overruled any human decision that aimed to thwart it. The reference to 'my people' is important. In spite of the division of the kingdom and the initial and continuing sin of the northern kingdom, God still regarded Israel as his people.

[1] The view that I have taken on this matter is in agreement with J. Niehaus, 'Amos,' pp. 462-63. For differing views of the translation, see E. Hammerschaimb, *The Book of Amos*, pp. 117-18; H. H. Rowley, 'Was Amos a Nabi?' *Festschrift Otto Eissfeldt* (Halle, 1947), pp. 191-98; James L. Mays, *Amos* (Old Testament Library: London: SCM Press, 1969), pp. 137-39; Gary Smith, *Amos, Obadiah, Jonah*, pp. 139-40.

16. Now therefore hear the word of the Lord*. 'You say, "Do not prophesy against Israel, and do not preach against the house of Isaac."'*

The response to Amaziah's demand is marked out by the words 'now therefore' (*vᵉʿattâh*), a standard phrase that indicates the following section is the consequence of the preceding one.[1] Even though speaking to just one man, Amos used the traditional introductory formula to the Lord's word: 'hear the word of the Lord.' The need of the hour was for Amaziah, and the people of Israel in general, to hear what God was declaring through his prophet. Such hearing was not just listening to the sound of the words, but taking to heart the message conveyed by them. 'You say' (*'âttâh 'omêr*) is a participial construction that would embrace the idea of repetitions of this message. 'You are saying,' or 'You keep on saying,' are possible translations. Amaziah's message is repeated in like form to verse 13, but with the addition: 'and do not preach against the house of Isaac.' The verb for preaching (*nâtaf*, hi.) is not a common word, but it has the sense of 'drip' or 'flow.' It occurs with its metaphorical meaning of prophesying or preaching (letting words flow) five times in Micah (Mic. 2:6 thrice; 2:11 twice), twice in Ezekiel (Ezek. 21:2, 7), and here in Amos 7:16. It may have been used with a derogatory implication here, implying that the prophet was just emitting a flow of words (see NEB, 'go drivelling on'), but its use in Ezekiel shows that it could be employed in the sense of a stream of speech. While Israel has been called 'Jacob' three times already (6:8; 7:2, 5), this is the only occurrence in which it is called 'Isaac' (see its use earlier in the context in verse 9).

17. *'Therefore thus says the* Lord*: "Your wife shall be a prostitute in the city, and your sons and your daughters shall fall by the sword, and your land shall be divided up with a measuring line; you your-*

[1] *IBHS*, p. 667, 39.3.4f.

self shall die in an unclean land, and Israel shall surely go into exile away from its land.'"'

'Therefore' (*lâkên*) points to the consequences awaiting Israel. While Amos was the spokesman, the verdict was that of the LORD: 'Thus says the LORD.' The LORD's message has been given consistently throughout the book, though with increasing specification. Earlier pointers to the impending exile had been given, but now the fullest statement of it follows. First of all, indication is given of what was going to happen to Amaziah and his family. While his sons and daughters would perish by the sword, his wife 'shall be a prostitute.' This may indicate that she will be so destitute that the only way she can exist will be by becoming a harlot. Invasion would have consequences for the land as well: 'your land shall be divided up.' Some of the language of the occupancy of Canaan and its division among the tribes is now used of the captors breaking it up in parcels, presumably so that rewards could be given to the victorious warriors. It is likely that the chief priest at Bethel must have had considerable possessions, including land that the family is to lose. The worst fate, however, is for Amaziah himself. He is to be deported to 'an unclean country,' a pagan one. There ritual purity could not be maintained. The final word from the prophet, 'and Israel shall surely go into exile, away from its land,' is the exact repetition of what Amaziah had reported to the king regarding Amos' message (see verse 11). Confrontation did not cause Amos to change his message. It remained exactly the same.

Application

God's words often cause confrontation between the messenger and the audience. Numerous biblical examples demonstrate this, including the opposition that the Lord Jesus himself faced in his ministry (see, for example, Matt.

15:12; 21:23-27, 45; Mark 6:1-6; John 8:42-58). Our human and sinful mindset is challenged by the truth, and naturally rebels against it. With darkened hearts our thinking becomes futile and we want to exchange the truth of God for a lie (Rom. 1:21, 25). Old Testament prophets, New Testament apostles, and preachers today face the same situation. The truth hurts. Amos is an example of a prophet who, when challenged about his uncomfortable message regarding the nation and the king, did not alter his message. What had been reported about him was confirmed by the prophet himself. Hostile responses to the truth are to be met by its repetition, not its substitution by another gospel (Gal. 1:6-9).

5. *The Fourth Vision—A Basket of Summer Fruits (8:1-3)*

1. *This is what the Lord GOD showed me: behold a basket of summer fruit.*

The next vision is introduced with exactly the same language as the three visions in chapter 7 (with the exception of the change of subject to 'he' in the third one): 'This is what the Lord GOD showed me: behold, ...' On this occasion the vision concerned summer fruit.

2. *And he said, 'Amos, what do you see?' And I said, 'A basket of summer fruit.' Then the LORD said to me, 'The end has come upon my people Israel; I will never again pass by them.'*

The opening words are a repetition of the question that Amos was asked in the third vision in chapter 7 (verse 8). After Amos gives the answer, 'a basket of summer fruit' (*k^{e}lûv qáyits*, lit. 'a basket of summer [fruit],' the LORD's response involves a play on words: 'The end has come upon my people Israel,' involving the Hebrew word *qayits*, 'basket,' and *qêts*, 'end.' It is significant that the word *qêts* occurred in the 10th-century BC document, the Geza calendar.[1] It lists among the months of the year, 'the month of summer fruits' (*yerach qêts*), a usage that *DCH* calls a by-form of *qáyits*.[2] The play on words between *qayits* and *qêts* may well have been common before Amos' time. The message is that finality has come to Israel, for she is ripe for judgment. The final declaration, 'I will never again pass by them,' is a repetition of a phrase that has been used already in 7:8 (see comments on that verse). All God's acts of compassion will cease (see 7:3, 6) for he has decreed the destruction of Israel as a nation.

> 3. *'The songs of the temple shall become wailings in that day,' declares the Lord GOD. 'So many dead bodies!' 'They are thrown everywhere!' 'Silence!'*

The LORD's message relates to 'the day of the LORD,' first introduced in 5:18 (see commentary). Judgment is at hand for Israel, and the response to it is given in the words: 'the songs in the temple shall become wailings.' Some have suggested that instead of 'songs' (*shîrôt*), the plural feminine form should be translated 'female singers.' However, a singular feminine form for 'song' (*shîrâh*) does occur (see, for example, Deut. 31:30; Psa. 18:1; Isa. 5:1), and though the plural is unattested elsewhere, there is no good reason to reject it here. The explanation for this response follows: '"So many dead bodies!"—"They are thrown everywhere."' The vision is of dead bodies thrown around in every place. Whether they have died because of enemy brutality or because of the plague is not specified. The description is very similar to that in 6:10. The command 'Silence' may be an abbreviated form of the expression that occurred earlier in 6:10: 'Silence! We must not mention the name of the LORD.'

[1] For the Hebrew text, see J. C. L. Gibson, *Textbook of Syrian Semitic Inscriptions*, vol. 1, pp. 3-4. The English translation is in *DOTT*, pp. 201-2.

[2] *DCH*, VII, p. 278.

6. *Declarations against Greedy Merchants (8:4-6)*

> 4. *Hear this, you who trample on the needy and bring the poor of the land to an end,*

A special word is directed to one group in Israel. The command, 'Hear this' (*shimᵉʿû zoʾt*), may well carry some emphasis, and it was a standard form used by other prophets as well (see Hos. 5:1; Joel 1:2). It does not seem to differ from the formula used earlier, 'Hear this word' (*shimᵉʿû ʾet haddâvâr hazzeh*). The accusation, 'you who trample on the needy and bring the poor of the land to an end,' is very like the one already presented against Israel in 2:7. There the accusation is that the oppression is against 'the poor' (*dallîm*) and 'the afflicted' (*ʿanâvîm*), whereas here it is against 'the poor' (*ʾevyôn*) and 'the needy of the land' (*ʿanivvê ʾârets*). The participle 'trample' (*shoʾafîm*) was also used in 2:7, to which is added here that they bring to an end the poor of the land. The verb used is the causative form of the verb 'to cease or stop' (*shâvat*, hi.), with the following verses specifying the way that the poor will be destroyed.

> 5, 6. *saying, 'When will the new moon be over, that we may sell grain? And the Sabbath, that we may offer wheat for sale, that we may make the ephah small and the shekel great and deal deceitfully with false balances, that we may buy the poor for silver and the needy for a pair of sandals and sell the chaff of the wheat?'*

The focus of the message concentrates on dishonest commercial practices. 'The new moon' translates a Hebrew word (*chódesh*) that can be rendered by 'month,' 'monthly,' or 'new moon.' The start of the month was one of the appointed feast days, and it is stated in 2 Chronicles 8:13 to involve burnt offerings. Psalm 81:3 confirms this, adding that the trumpets were blown on that day. So anxious were people in Amos' time to get on with matters of businesses, that they eagerly looked for this festive occasion to be over so that they could resume trading their grain.[1] Likewise, for them the Sabbath restricted their business of selling wheat, so they wanted it to end as quickly as possible. The Hebrew that the ESV renders 'that we may offer wheat for sale' is literally, 'that we may open wheat,' i.e., that we may open the stores of wheat. Five dishonest practices are then listed, starting with 'that we may make the ephah small,' adjusting the expected amount in an ephah (approx. 40 litres). The corollary was that they were 'making the shekel great,' that is, adjusting the weight of the shekel that was used as currency so that the price was boosted. In addition, they were dealing 'deceitfully with false balances.' Elsewhere in the Old Testament this practice was labelled as being an abomination to the LORD (Prov. 11:1). Others were being defrauded through their malpractice. The fourth sin in this list is that they were buying 'the poor for silver.' This meant that the poor became so impoverished by having to pay what amounted to inflated prices, that finally they had no recourse but to sell themselves into slavery. Similar language has been used already in 2:6 (see comments there). Though sandals were sometimes used in property transactions (Ruth 4:7, 8), no implication is given here that any transfer of property was in question. It is simply that poverty had driven people to such lengths. The final practice that is condemned is that the rich were 'sell[ing] the chaff of the wheat.' This involved mixing the husks of the grain (*mappal*, lit. 'fallings,' 'refuse') with other grain, and thereby adding to the impoverishment of the poor.

[1] The phrase 'that we may offer wheat for sale' involves a cognate accusative. The verb is *shâvar*, hi. 'to sell [grain],' while the thing being sold is *shéver*, 'grain.' The connection between *shâvar* I, '*to break*,' and *shâvar* II, '*to sell*,' is uncertain. It is also an illustration of a Hebrew cohortative form being used in a dependent clause following a question. For this grammatical point, see *IBHS*, p. 575, 34.5.2.

7. *The Lord's Oath against the Greedy Merchants (8:7-10)*

> 7. *The Lord has sworn by the pride of Jacob: 'Surely I will never forget any of their deeds.'*

The judgment on the rich is enforced by a solemn oath, sworn 'by the pride of Jacob.' Twice earlier in this book of Amos mention is made of God swearing oaths. The first one in 4:2 said that he swore 'by his holiness' (*b*[e]*qodshô*) while in the other, in 6:8, he swore 'by himself' (*b*[e]*nafshô*, lit. 'by his soul'). 'The pride of Jacob' is not a reference to Jacob's attitude to himself, but rather to the object of Jacob's confidence—the Lord. Use of 'the pride of Jacob' to refer to God is similar to the expression 'the glory' that is similarly employed in Psalm 106:20 and Jeremiah 2:11 (see the echo of this usage in Rom. 1:23, '[they] exchanged the glory of the immortal God'). The content of the oath is: 'Surely I will never forget any of their deeds.' Judgment on the rich was certain because God's knowledge was all-embracive. All their sinful actions, small and great, were known to him and would evoke his punishment.

> 8. *'Shall not the land tremble on this account, and everyone mourn who dwells in it, and all of it rise like the Nile, and be tossed about and sink again, like the Nile of Egypt?'*

The opening clause is marked in Hebrew by the use of the particle (*ha-*) to indicate a question, but this marker appears to do duty also for the second clause as well. The question expects a positive answer. The words 'on this account' are a reference back to what has been described in verses 4-6. The verb 'tremble' is used elsewhere for the shaking of the earth by an earthquake (1 Sam. 14:15), and clearly this is what is in view here. The disaster that Amos has been speaking about throughout this book is pictured as being an earthquake, with the inhabitants in mourning. 'To mourn' is used elsewhere in Old

Testament poetry to depict the results of drought or devastation (Isa. 24:7; 33:9; Joel 1:10). The coming calamity is, therefore, also likened to the annual rising and falling of the waters of the Nile.[1] No evidence exists of any Egyptian sojourn by Amos, but the facts concerning the Nile must have been widely known in the Near East. The verbs, 'be tossed about' (*nigr^eshâh*) and 'sink' (*nishq^ehâ*), are graphic descriptions of the uproar that is coming upon Israel. The same analogy will be used again in 9:5.

> 9. *'And on that day,' declares the Lord* G*OD*, *'I will make the sun go down at noon and darken the earth in broad daylight.'*

This verse commences a series of oracles that are introduced either by the phrase 'in that day' (*bayyôm hahû'*, 8:9, 13; 9:11), or by the words, 'the days are coming' (*yâmîm bâ'îm*, 8:11; 9:13). No great difference can be discerned between these expressions. Here, both point to impending judgment within the foreseeable future, not the far distant future. The section is notable for the repeated use of 'I will…' that occurs five times. In itself this repetition is a reminder of God's sovereignty that is going to be demonstrated in judgment. The opening expression, 'And on that day,' has the ring of epochal finality about it (see its use in Zech. 13:1). God is going to act decisively in bringing judgment on the land. Here the message is couched in terms of an eclipse. Other prophets also use this imagery as part of their depiction of coming judgment (see Isa. 13:10; Joel 2:10; 3:15), as Jesus, the last of the great prophets also did (Matt. 24:29). It is impossible to date Amos' ministry by any calculation of eclipse dates in the 8th century BC. Like other prophets, he is using a known phenomenon to add to this descrip-

[1] The word 'Nile' (y^e*'ôr*) is written defectively on the first occurrence here. In the phrase, 'like the Nile' (*kâ'ôr*), the consonant *yod* is missing, but in the later phrase, 'the river of Egypt,' it is present (*ky'ôr*). The same analogy is used in 9:5, and there the full form, *kay^e'ôr*, appears.

tion, and possibly also to draw upon the fear that eclipses often created.

10. *'I will turn your feasts into mourning and all your songs into lamentation; I will bring sackcloth on every waist and baldness on every head; I will make it like the mourning for an only son and the end of it like a bitter day.'*

Outward portents of God's judgment will also be accompanied by inner change. The 'feasts' were those associated with the three annual pilgrimage feasts (Passover, Feast of Weeks, Feast of Ingathering). The Hebrew for one of these feasts (*chag*) is, as we have noted before when commenting upon 5:21, parallel to the Arabic word for pilgrimage to Mecca (*hajj*). Instead of them being times of festal joy, the people will mourn, and even their singing will be altered to become dirges. The word for 'lamentation' (*qînâh*) is mainly employed in songs used in mourning rituals. The idea of lament is carried further by the clauses which follow: 'I will bring sackcloth on every waist and baldness on every head.' It was normal practice in Israel for mourners to wear sackcloth (Heb. *sak*, from whence comes the English word, 'sack'). It was usually made of goat's hair, and was dark in colour (see Rev. 6:12). It was also common to shave the head as a sign of the depth of grief a person was experiencing. The word used here for 'baldness' (*qorchâh*) occurs eleven times in the Old Testament, all in connection with mourning procedures. The divine initiative will extend further: 'I will make it like the mourning for an only son and the end of it like a bitter day.' The extent of the coming sorrow is likened to losing an only son, an analogy made all the more pointed as loss of an only son meant the loss of future generations. The expression 'the end of it' (*'ach^{a}rîtâh*) can be used in an eschatological sense of 'the last day,' and elsewhere in the prophetical writings it is linked with coming judgment (see Jer. 23:20; 30:24).

8. *The Threat of Famine (8:11-14)*

11. *'Behold, the days are coming,' declares the Lord God, 'when I will send a famine on the land—not a famine of bread, nor a thirst for water, but of hearing the words of the Lord.'*

The Hebrew text, 'behold,' 'see' (*hinnêh*) often marks out a dramatic development, in either the past or future. Here it is future, as the participle 'coming' (*bâ'îm*) indicates what is to follow.[1] 'The days are coming' seems to be used as a variant for 'in that day.' What is predicted is famine, not of literal food (called here 'bread') but spiritual food, 'a famine … of hearing the words of the Lord.' One of God's judgments is going to be the absence of prophetic ministry so that Israel will be bereft of a word from the Lord. This can be understood in two ways. It could refer to the fact that Israel in exile was not going to have the same type of prophetic ministry that had been carried out by prophets such as Hosea and Amos. The prophetic voice was to be stilled for Israel. The other possibility is that the message related to a cessation of prophetic activity leading up to the final judgment in 722 BC. The following verse suggests that the second interpretation is correct. While a famine leaving people destitute of food was dreadful, even more dreadful would be a famine of divine revelation.

12. *'They shall wander from sea to sea, and from north to east; they shall run to and fro, to seek the word of the Lord, but they shall not find it.'*

The reference to the points of the compass seems to confirm the interpretation of the previous verse. The picture is of people desperately trying to find a message from the Lord. Just as starving people hunt for food and water, so the people of Israel will ransack the

[1] For the usage of *hinnêh*, see *DIHG-S*, p. 91, §72, Rem. 4, and for its use along with a participle, p. 137, §113 (f).

country attempting to find God's word. The search will be 'from sea to sea' and 'from north to east.' These were standard expressions for west (the Mediterranean Sea) and east (the Dead Sea), and for north (Lebanon) and east (the Euphrates region). The inclusion of 'east' carried another message as well. It was from the east that the conqueror was going to come, just as Isaiah later told Judah concerning the coming of Cyrus ('from the east,' Isa. 41:2, 25). The search will be fruitless: 'but they shall not find it.' This too is God's judgment on the people. The Hebrew text has only, 'they will not find,' without the object being expressed, but the context makes plain what is intended. The same combination of seek/find occurs in Ecclesiastes 8:17, and Jesus used it as well (Matt. 7:7).

13. *'In that day the lovely virgins and the young men shall faint for thirst.'*

In continuing the message, the introductory words, 'In that day,' are used as in verse 9, without any alteration of the time frame for the coming judgment. 'The lovely virgins and the young men' represent the cream of the population. The word for 'women' (*b^{e}tûlâh* s., *b^{e}tûlot* pl.) may mean 'virgins' but more generally 'young marriageable women,' while the word for 'young men' (*bachûrîm*) comes from the verb 'to choose.' It can denote the choicest of young men, especially the ones selected to be warriors, though here in contrast with *b^{e}tûlot* it seems to have only a general meaning, 'young men.' Even those in the vigour of youth will be deeply affected by the absence of a word from the LORD. Their thirst will not be satisfied because there will be no further revelation for them.

14. *'Those who swear by the Guilt of Samaria, and say, "As your god lives, O Dan," and, "As the Way of Beersheba lives," they shall fall, and never rise again.'*

Some particular members of Israelite society are singled out for attention. Instead of taking oaths in the name of the LORD, they were swearing oaths in the name of particular local gods. The form of oath here was common in Israel (see, for example, 'As surely as you live,' 1 Sam. 1:26; 'As the LORD lives,' 1 Sam. 14:39) but the god to whom appeal was made was a substitute for the true God. One word associated with Samaria was 'guilt,' that is, it brought guilt on Samaria that the inhabitants did not celebrate the goodness and grace of the living God. An alternative view holds that the reference is to a female goddess called Ashima, while it has also been suggested that the word should be read as the name, Asherah (a Canaanite mother-goddess). However, the latter view not only needs alternate vocalisation of the Hebrew word but also the addition of another consonant, *r*. While the biblical text records that Jeroboam II had two golden calves made, setting up one in Bethel and the other in Dan (1 Kings 12:28-30), no further information is known of local gods that were worshipped at Beersheba. The mention of Dan is understandable as it was near the northern boundary of Israel, but Beersheba was deep into the territory of Judah. Amos, as a southerner, would know about it, but for the reference to hold any meaning for the recipients of the message, such knowledge must have been widespread. The final words, 'they shall fall, and never rise again,' are a definitive verdict on the false swearers. Their downfall was certain.

Application

Several thoughts flow out of this section. First, God did not predict the coming judgment in terms that allowed the people to work out with precision the time frame. It was just to be 'in that day' or, 'in those days.' Similarly, our Lord Jesus, in teaching about the end of the age, warned that false predictions of that time would be made (Mark 13:14-36). He encouraged his disciples: 'What do you see' (verses 23, 33) and 'Keep watch' (verse 35). Secondly, there is a danger worse than absence of food and water, and that is absence of God's word. The greatest disaster that anyone can have is for God to deny them access to his revelation. In his sovereignty God can leave people in their sin, 'Keep on hearing, but do not understand' (Isa. 6:9; Mark 4:11, 12; Acts 28:25-29). Thirdly, God does not simply allow the world to wander along, creating its own destiny. He is actively working out his purposes today just as he was in Amos' time.

9. *The Fifth Vision—The* Lord *in His Glory (9:1-4)*

1a. *I saw the* Lord *standing beside the altar, and he said: 'Strike the capitals until the thresholds shake, and shatter them on the heads of all the people.'*

This is the introduction to a remarkable vision. Just as Isaiah had a revelation of the Lord on his throne (Isa. 6:1), Amos saw him in the temple, a visionary temple. God had taken his place by the temple altar, and gave a command that its destruction should commence. The effect of a blow on 'the capitals' would be felt even as far as the foundations. The destruction of the real temple at Bethel was to take place during the Assyrian invasion, and God's hand was behind that occurrence. His eyes were on the people for evil, not for good (see comment on verse 4b).

Several features of this vision are striking.

1. Verses 1a-4 are framed by introductory and concluding statements (verses 1b and 4b). The opening statement is a command to kill the people with the sword, and the theme is repeated in verse 4b.

2. The central section of the vision contains a series of clauses all beginning with the Hebrew word *'im* ('though') and concluding

with the declaration in verse 4b that God's eyes are on the people for evil, and not for good.

3. The pattern of these central statements is formalised:

Though they [dig down, climb up, etc], from there I will [bring them down, hunt them down, etc].

The only exception to this is verse 2a where 'my hand' serves as a substitute for the first-personal pronoun.

4. There is music to the ear in this piece, as the consonant *shin* (pronounced like the English 'sh') appears eleven times (verse 2, four times; verse 3, five times; verse 4, twice). In addition two other 's' sounds occur, *samek* in verse 1 (*yânûs, nâs*) and verse 3 (*yissât^{e}rû*), and sin in verse 3b (*'^{a}chappês*) and verse 4b (*v^{e}samtî*), and also *tsade* occurs in verse 4b (*'^{a}tstsavveh*, twice).

5. Twice reference is made to death by the sword (*b^{e}chérev*), in both cases with the verb 'to kill' (*hârag*).

> 1b. *'and those who are left of them I will kill with the sword; not one of them shall flee away; not one of them shall escape.'*

The consequences of invasion by the Assyrians are spelt out in graphic terms. None in Israel should have had misconceptions about the result of the Assyrian incursion into their land. For many, it was not going to be captivity and exile but rather death. This is given even greater emphasis by the declaration: 'not one of them shall flee away; not one of them shall escape.' The syntax of these statements is identical, and consonance and assonance also make them memorable. A fairly literal translation is: 'They will not have one fleeing who will flee, or an escapee who will escape' (*lo' yânûs lâhem nâs, lo' yimmâlêt lâhem pâlît*).[1] The point of the message is that even those who think they can escape God's judgment will find that they will be overtaken by it.

[1] The consonance is that in both clauses an imperfect of a verb is followed by the active participle of the same verb (*yânûs / nâs*; *yimmâlêt / pâlît*). The assonance is that there is repetition of the same or similar sounds (*-â*, six times; *ûs / nâs*; *-lêt / -lît*).

2. *'If they dig into Sheol, from there shall my hand take them; if they climb up to heaven, from there I will bring them down.'*

The next few verses are marked by the use of obvious and extravagant exaggeration. This hyperbole gives greater vividness to the imagery. The first two of the rhyming statements make the contrast between Sheol, or possibly, the depths of the grave, with the height of the heavens. The preference is to retain the MT text and accept that the Hebrew word *sh^e'ol* occurs here in poetry for the more common word for 'grave,' *qéver.*[1] The verbs used in the second part of the verse, 'climb up' (*'âlâh*) and 'bring down' (*yârad*, hi.) form a fixed pair, and are used together in poetry (see their use in Isa. 14:14, 15; Jer. 48:5; Psa. 104:8). The point in either situation is that there is no escape from the Lord. From the one, his hand can lift them out, while from the other, he can bring them down. The main thought is the impossibility of escaping from God. It is very close to the expressions in Psalm 139: 'If I ascend to heaven, you are there! If I make my bed in Sheol, you are there! If I take the wings of the morning and dwell in the uttermost parts of the sea, even there your hand shall lead me, and your right hand shall hold me' (verses 8-10).

3. *'If they hide themselves on the top of Carmel, from there I will search them out and take them; and if they hide from my sight at the bottom of the sea, there I will command the serpent, and it shall bite them.'*

Carmel is one of the loftiest places in Israel. It begins near the present day city of Haifa, and is not just a single mount but rather a range running south-east. The vision is of people trying to scale

[1] For excellent discussions on *sh^e'ol*, see R. L. Harris, *TWOT*, 2, pp. 892-93, and 'Why *Sh^e'ol* was translated "Grave,"' *The Making of a Contemporary Translation: The Purpose and Method of the New International Version*, ed. Kenneth Barker (London: Hodder & Stoughton, 1987), pp. 75-92.

Carmel and hide there. It is noted for its caves, which were once dwelling places. The implication is that it would take more effort to locate them there, for the Lord's word is: 'I will search them out and take them.' The verb to search (*châpas*) is used elsewhere of Saul seeking out David (1 Sam. 23:23), and of God searching out the wicked of Jerusalem (Zeph. 1:12). Hence, it is clearly a fitting descriptive term for God's actions in seeking out for capture those trying to flee from him. Even hiding 'at the bottom of the sea' would not be able to ensure that they would be insulated from God's all-seeing eyes. There he would issue the command to the serpent to bite them. The word for 'serpent' (*nâchâsh*) has been used already in 5:19 of God's judgment. No indication exists in this passage of a link with 'Leviathan,' the associate of the Canaanite sea-god Yam.

> 4. *'And if they go into captivity before their enemies, there I will command the sword, and it shall kill them; and I will fix my eyes upon them for evil and not for good.'*

Once more the message that Amos was delivering focuses on exile. The thought of being alienated from Canaan was never pleasant, but Amos' words here combine the idea of them being taken from their land and 'if they go into captivity before their enemies.' To exile was added the prospect of cruelty by the Assyrians in their driving them away into captivity. If Amos' hearers and readers thought that at least their lives would be preserved as captives, the message indicates that the Lord could even bring the punishment of death on them there. It is not just natural death in an exilic environment but a cruel and violent death by 'the sword.' The final words of verse 4 point to God's intention for Israel. He will fix his eyes 'upon them for evil and not for good.' These words may be an echo of the story of Joseph in Genesis. When Joseph finally made himself known to his brothers, he declared that what they had done to him was intended for evil but, in preserving the family through him, God had meant it for good (Gen. 50:20).

Application

Yet again the message Amos was bringing to Israel spoke of the power of the living God. He is able to smash great buildings like the temple. Also, nothing can be hidden from him. Wherever we go, he is able to search us out and fulfil his plan for us, and at times that plan may not be to our liking. He weaves our web of time with mercy and with judgment. His character and works challenge us to acknowledge his authority over our lives. We are called to sing:

Not unto us, O Lord of heav'n,
But to Your name be glory given:
In love and truth, Lord, you fulfil
The counsels of Your sovereign will.
Though nations fail Your pow'r to own,
Yet, Lord, You reign, and You alone.

Psalm 115:1, Trinity Hymnal 1961.

10. *A Doxology Proclaiming the* LORD*'s Might (9:5, 6)*

The narrative of God's judgments upon Israel is interrupted by a doxology that extols his might. It is the third and final doxology in the book (for the earlier ones see 4:13; 5:8, 9). This adds to the context because it reinforces the lesson that God is well able to fulfil his purposes. He who controls the natural world has the power to bring judgment on his people.

5. *The Lord* GOD *of hosts, he who touches the earth and it melts, and all who dwell in it mourn, and all of it rises like the Nile, and sinks again, like the Nile of Egypt.*

The designation of God is different though close to ones that had already been used earlier in the book (see especially the comments on 3:13). 'The Lord God of hosts' is a combination of 'Lord' (*'ᵃdonay*), *yhwh*, and 'the hosts' (*hatstsᵉvâ'ôt*). God's authority over creation is shown by the way he 'touches the earth and it melts.' God's touch is always authoritative. He touches men (1 Kings 19:7), sacrifices (Judg. 6:21), and, as here, mountains (Psa. 104:32). Elsewhere God's voice causes the earth to melt (Psa. 46:6). The translation 'melt' may not be the best English equivalent of the Hebrew verb *mûg*. It may be better to adopt 'shake' or 'wave.'[1] The description of touching and melting is simply an expression of the outworking of omnipotence. The effect is expressed in poetic terms: 'and all who dwell in it mourn.' Just like those who mourn over the dead, so the earth's inhabitants respond with an outburst of grief. The part that follows is almost identical to 8:8 (see comments), a statement of the uproar caused as God administers his judgments.

> 6. *who builds his upper chambers in the heavens and founds his vault upon the earth; who calls for the waters of the sea and pours them out upon the surface of the earth—the* Lord *is his name.*

The message continues with a poetic description of creation. God is the builder who fashioned the heavens, calling them his habitation. He is also the one who sets the foundations of the earth. Whereas the doxology started with a long title for God, it finishes with the brief statement: 'the Lord is his name.' It is the covenantal God of Israel who is all-powerful.

[1] See *DCH*, V, p. 170.

11. The Continuation of the Judgment Pronouncement (9:7-10)

7. *'Are you not like the Cushites to me, O people of Israel?' declares the* LORD. *'Did I not bring up Israel from the land of Egypt, and the Philistines from Caphtor and the Syrians from Kir?'*

Israel needed to know that other nations had also seen God's hand at work in shaping their destiny. Israel's God was the God of the nations, and he directed their history as well. The verse contains two questions from the LORD to his people. The first one is: 'Are you not like the Cushites to me, O people of Israel? ' The people of Israel thought that God's concern was centred on themselves. Now he disabuses them of this by indicating that he had the same interest in the people of Cush, who were one of the most distant peoples known in Israel. Cush was probably the area south and east of Egypt, though it may have included southern Arabia, which is only separated from that region by a narrow strip of water. God was involved in more than the exodus of Israel from Egypt. Did he not bring 'the Philistines from Caphtor and the Syrians from Kir?' Of course, he brought the Philistines to Palestine from Crete,[1] and the Syrians from Kir, whose location was somewhere in Mesopotamia (see comment on 1:5). There is a parallel between the forced return of the Arameans to Kir by Ahaz (2 Kings 16:9) and the Israelites' fear of being sent back to Egypt (Deut. 17:16; 28:68). The point here is that it was not only Israel who had had an exodus experience, for the Philistines and the Syrians had both been involved in an exodus under God's sovereign hand.

8. *'Behold, the eyes of the Lord* GOD *are upon the sinful kingdom, and I will destroy it from the surface of the ground, except that I will not utterly destroy the house of Jacob,' declares the* LORD.

[1] The English word 'Palestine' is simply a corruption from 'Philistine.'

The resumed judgment picture begins with a word to get the attention of hearers and readers: 'Look!' (*hinnêh*; ESV 'behold' is too weak).[1] Using anthropomorphic language, the declaration is given that the Sovereign Lord knows the character of the people of Israel. They form a 'sinful kingdom' in his sight. Individual sections of the community have earlier been characterised in the book as being sinful, but now the whole nation is described in this way. This part of the verse is in the third-person, but suddenly a switch is made and the words that follow are a declaration in the first-person of God's intended action: 'I will destroy it.'[2] The penalty for this is a divine act of destruction 'from the surface of the ground.' In the Old Testament it is not only the destruction caused by the flood which is said to have been from the face of the earth, but other divine judgments as well (see, e.g., Exod. 32:12; 1 Sam. 20:15; 1 Kings 9:7; Jer. 28:16). Israel now faces that same type of annihilation. But a word of promise and reassurance follows: '"except that I will not utterly destroy the house of Jacob," declares the Lord.' The introductory 'except' (Heb. *'efes kî*) places a restriction on the preceding clause. In spite of the threat of such total judgment, nevertheless, in the process not all the house of Jacob will be destroyed.[3] Jacob has already been referred to several times earlier in Amos (3:13; 6:8; 7:2, 5; 8:7). 'The house of Jacob' is a synonym for 'the house of Israel' (as in the following verse). Probably these expressions are intended to indicate the whole family of Israel, particularly the southerners in Judah who, while not being called 'Israel,' were indeed the legitimate family of Israel. In these words, as in the reference to the fallen booth of David (verse 11), there was a rebuke for the Israel of Amos' day. Whatever its claims, Israel did not constitute fully the people of God. As so often in this book, a final confirmation is given that this message is indeed from the Lord.

[1] See previous comment on hinnêh, p. 140 n.1.

[2] While this type of switch is unusual in Western poetry, it is quite common in the poetry of the Old Testament.

[3] *IBHS*, pp. 672-73.

9. *'For behold, I will command, and shake the house of Israel among all the nations as one shakes with a sieve, but no pebble shall fall to the earth.'*

A time in the future is coming when, by divine command, a sifting of Israel will occur. Several English versions simply commence this verse with 'for,' but that is not strong enough. The Hebrew text says: 'For, behold, I am about to command …' (*kî hinnêh 'ânokî m^e^tsavveh*).[1] The presence of 'for behold' and the emphatic 'I' (*'ânokî*) draw attention to divine intervention in scattering the people without completely destroying the nation. God's reassurance is: 'I will … shake the house of Israel among all the nations as one shakes with a sieve.' The imagery is that of sifting grain through a sieve, though the word for 'corn' is not in the Hebrew text. It is literally, 'as one shakes with a sieve.' The word translated 'sieve' (*k^e^vârâh*) only occurs here in the Old Testament. Similarly in the final clause, 'but no pebble shall fall to the earth,' the Hebrew word *ts^e^rôr* is also a rare word, and of dubious origin. Rather than something like 'ear,' it is more likely 'pebble,'[2] and thus the idea is that while grain is retained in the sieve, any other material fails to fall through the opening. A dispersion of Israel, seed sown among the nations, is going to take place, but sinners will not escape God's judgment. However, a remnant will be preserved. The people, as a whole, had to realise that a divinely initiated separation was going to take place.

10. *All the sinners of my people shall die by the sword, who say, 'Disaster shall not overtake or meet us.'*

The theme of 'pebbles' continues in this verse. Those who remain obstinately opposed to the LORD will be judged by him. They are

[1] For the use of the participle in Heb. in the sense of 'about to,' 'going to,' see *IBHS*, pp. 627-28, 37.6.e; and, R. J. Williams, *Hebrew Syntax: An Outline*, p. 39, §214.

[2] See *NIDOTTE*, 3, p. 842; and *DCH*, VII, p. 160.

'the sinners of my people.' The message is that not all of those belonging outwardly to Israel were really part of his people. This is the principle that the Apostle Paul develops in Romans 2:28, 29. In the coming invasion by the Assyrians they 'shall die by the sword,' a repetition of what has been said already earlier in this chapter (see verses 1 and 4). These are the same people who assert: 'Disaster shall not overtake or meet us.' That is to say, there are those in Israel who claim that their privileges will exempt them from God's judgment. How mistaken they are, for they will not escape the disaster that is coming!

Application

One of the lessons that Israel was slow to learn was that their God, the Sovereign LORD, was concerned with other nations as well. He had called the Arameans and the Philistines, not savingly, but by his common grace. His discriminating grace was, however, persistently evident towards Israel, and in this passage there is a hope that Israel will not be totally destroyed. God's people in any age cannot boast of what they are in themselves, but only what they are because of his grace towards them. In love he predestines people to adoption, in accordance with his pleasure and will (Eph. 1:4, 5). We as believers have to join Robert Murray M'Cheyne (1813–1842) when he wrote:

Chosen not for good in me,
Wakened up from wrath to flee,
Hidden in the Saviour's side,
By the Spirit sanctified,
Teach me, Lord, on earth to show
By my love how much I owe.

'When This Passing World Is Done.'

6

Epilogue: Israel's Eventual Restoration (9:11-15)

1. *Restoration of the Davidic Dynasty (9:11, 12)*

While hints have been given earlier in Amos regarding hope for Israel's future, this passage at the very end of the book makes it clear that a new day was going to dawn for them. God will take the initiative in a work of restoration (note the number of times that '*I*' occurs).

> 11. *'In that day I will raise up the booth of David that is fallen and repair its breaches, and raise up its ruins and rebuild it as in the days of old.'*

This passage has many remarkable features to it.[1] The first is the time frame in which the events are to happen. 'In that day,' says the prophet. This phrase can be used of events near at hand, but specifically it often denotes a time still ahead. The prophets often use it, even when they themselves may have been unsure about the actual fulfilment time. They 'searched and inquired carefully, inquiring

[1] For a very helpful discussion on verses 11, 12, and their use in Acts 15:16-18, see Walter C. Kaiser, Jr., 'The Davidic Promise and the Inclusion of the Gentiles (Amos 9:9-15 and Acts 15:13-18): A Test Passage for Theological Systems,' *JETS* 20 (1977), pp. 97-111.

what person or time the Spirit of Christ in them was indicating' (1 Pet. 1:10, 11). It is possible that the intention here is to indicate that the restoration will commence with the return from exile and continue on through to the time of the Messiah.[1] The promise is given that God is going to 'raise up the booth of David that is fallen,' a promise very similar in meaning to the message of Isaiah that Cyrus was going to rebuild Jerusalem (Isa. 44:26). The word translated 'raise up' (*qûm*, hi.) is regularly used of building or rebuilding.[2] First, this is a word of rebuke to Israel. In rejecting Rehoboam as king (1 Kings 12:16), they had shown that they despised the Davidic family. Now they are called on to acknowledge that future blessing will only come through the Davidic line. Secondly, use of 'booth,' 'tent' (*sukkâh*) is unexpected, as just a few verses previously 'house of Jacob' (verse 8) and 'house of Israel' (verse 9) have been used, and the reference could well have been to the 'house of David,' as in 2 Samuel 7:26, 29. The added problem is the addition of the participle 'fallen' or 'falling' (*hannofélet*). It could refer to the division of the kingdom, a tragic event that lived on in the memory of the people (see Isa. 7:17, 'such days as have not come since the day that Ephraim departed from Judah'). However, the use of the participle points more to a situation in existence in Amos' time. This would be a reference to the tottering state of the Davidic dynasty, a monarchy with great prospects but that was marred by the sinfulness of its founder and his successors. Another factor that deserves attention is that a 'booth' was a temporary dwelling erected for use during the Feast of Booths or Tabernacles (Deut. 16:13-15) in order to remind the people of the wilderness experience. When Jeroboam I appointed the feast of tabernacles in imitation of the lawful one in Judah a month earlier, he stood and sacrificed at the altar (see 1 Kings 12:32, and also Lev. 23:33, 34). It is possible that the king had an important role to play at the Feast of Booths.

[1] For this interpretation, see T. E. McComiskey, 'Amos,' p. 329.

[2] See *DCH*, VII, p. 233b.

Hence, when this message of Amos is considered, it may well point to an expectation that the decrepit state of the Davidic dynasty will one day be replaced by a Davidic messiah, who would be a priest/ king.[1]

The message continues by designating three things that the LORD is to do: 'repair its breaches, and raise up its ruins and rebuild it as in the days of old.' The first verb only occurs seven times in the Old Testament, while the second and third appear very commonly (*qûm*, *c.* 470 times; *bânâh*, *c.* 370 times). A difficulty that is immediately apparent is that three different suffixes appear in the Hebrew text, as shown in the following literal translation: 'I will repair their (third pers. masc. pl.) broken places, restore his (third pers. masc. sing.) ruins, and build her (third pers. fem. sing.) as she used to be.' The LXX makes all the suffixes third-person feminine singular, but the Hebrew manuscripts preserve the variation. The general meaning is plain, in that restoration is going to occur for the Davidic family, or else the Davidic city of Jerusalem, and switching among pronouns is not uncommon in biblical Hebrew. In a general expression, the first Hebrew suffix ('their') probably refers back to broken city walls, while the second ('his') refers back to David, or else to his walls, which represent the Davidic dynasty. The final suffix ('her') is best taken as referring to the feminine word 'tent' (*sukkâh*). The phrase 'rebuild it as in the days of old' appears to be a reference to what the Davidic family had become through God's promises to David (2 Sam. 7:8-16). The promise is that David's hut, i.e., the Davidic dynasty, will be restored.

12. *'that they may possess the remnant of Edom and all the nations who are called by my name,' declares the* LORD *who does this.*

[1] I am here following the interpretation of J. A. Motyer, *The Day of the Lion*, pp. 202-3.

The message goes on to refer to one of the major enemies of Israel, Edom. No indication is given in the text of the identity of the subject of the verb 'possess.' In the context 'they' must be the Davidic dynasty or the Davidic kingdom. The joining together of David and Edom recalls David's conquest of Edom (2 Sam. 8:14), whereby the Edomites became David's vassals. Later Edom was an independent nation, though it was in conflict with Judah during the days of King Amaziah (2 Kings 14:7; 2 Chron. 25:5-14). The promise is that once more Edom will be subject to the Davidic family, for the LORD declares, 'and all the nations who are called by my name.' 'To bear the name' of someone was to acknowledge ownership or possession. God's name was called over Israel (Deut. 28:10), but here it is called over Gentiles (Heb. *gôyîm*). While active missionary work may not have been part of Israel's mission in the Old Testament, certainly the prospect is held out regarding the incorporation of Gentiles into God's family (see Psa. 67:3-5; 96:1-13). The message here is that there is going to be a future incorporation of Gentiles into the Davidic kingdom. As usual, the message is rounded off by the declaration that it is indeed a word from the LORD. To this is added the description that he is the one 'who does this.' What human effort could not accomplish, divine power will.

These words of Amos were quoted by James in the meeting of the Jerusalem assembly, as set out in Acts 15. In the discussion relating to allowing Gentiles to join the church without submitting to circumcision, James quotes from Amos. He was agreeing with Peter's words 'how God first visited the Gentiles, to take from them a people for his name' (Acts 15:14). The discussion on this quotation commences with variations from the MT.[1] Leaving aside the technicalities of James' use of the LXX text instead of the MT, the

[1] For an introduction to the questions, see Michael A. Braun, 'James' Use of Amos at the Jerusalem Council: Steps Toward a Possible Solution of the Textual and Theological Problems,' *JETS* 20 (1977), pp. 113-19.

main point remains clear. God's intention was always that Gentiles would be called into his kingdom (see Isa. 2:2-4; 11:10; 45:22-24; Zech. 14:16; Mal. 1:11). The inclusion of the Gentiles in the New Testament church was a fulfilment of that purpose.[1]

2. *Restoration of Israel (9:13-15)*

The prophecy of Amos ends on the note of the reinstatement of Israel in Canaan, in a new Eden. The picture is of restoration to an idyllic situation, in which there would be abundance of produce and security for the future.

> 13. *'Behold, the days are coming,' declares the* Lord, *'when the ploughman shall overtake the reaper and the treader of grapes him who sows the seed; the mountains shall drip sweet wine, and all the hills shall flow with it.'*

Instead of 'in that day' (verse 11), the continued message commences with 'the days are coming,' as in 8:11. No disjunction of future time is intended by this. The picture is of miraculous provision of food for the returnees. No time gap will exist between planting and reaping. The reaper will actually catch up with the sower. Furthermore, such abundance of grapes will result in new wine flowing from the mountains and hills. The same verb, 'drip' (Heb. *nâtaf*, hi.), occurs in a similar description in Joel 3:18: 'And in that day the mountains shall drip sweet wine, and the hills shall flow with milk.'

> 14. *'I will restore the fortunes of my people Israel, and they shall rebuild the ruined cities and inhabit them; they shall plant*

[1] For further discussion on the New Testament passage in question, good discussions can be found in F. F. Bruce, *The Acts of the Apostles: Greek Text with Introduction and Commentary*, 3rd ed. (Grand Rapids: Eerdmans, 1990), pp. 338-41; and I. H. Marshall, *Acts: An Introduction and Commentary, Tyndale NT Commentaries* (Leicester: Inter-Varsity Press, 1980), pp. 251-53.

vineyards and drink their wine, and they shall make gardens and eat their fruit.'

Words of promise and reassurance are given. The LORD's message is directed to 'my people Israel.' In spite of Israel's sin and subsequent banishment to exile in Assyria, they still remain his people, for the covenantal bond remains. The ESV rendering, 'the fortunes of my people' (also occurring as an alternative translation in the NIV), is not convincing, as similar phrases occur elsewhere in the sense of restoration from exile.[1] Restoration will involve resettlement with all its problems of rebuilding towns that were devastated and abandoned. New vineyards will also have to be planted so that there will be an abundance of wine, while the produce of the gardens will nourish the returnees. This verse continues the picture of paradise regained.

15. *'I will plant them on their land, and they shall never again be uprooted out of the land that I have given them,' says the LORD your God.*

The agricultural analogies continue with reference to planting and uprooting. Now it is not plants but people that are in view. Language is also borrowed from earlier in the Old Testament in passages in which God is the one who 'gave' Canaan to his people (see Deut. 1:8, 21; 3:18; 4:21; Josh. 1:6, 11). The imagery is of plants securely placed in the ground with no prospect that someone would come along and uproot them. The initiative is with God ('*I* will plant'), and he will ensure the preservation of Israel. The picture is not of a literal return to Palestine with uninterrupted rights of occupancy there. Rather, it is of an eschatological event when the LORD will indeed gather exiled people into the security of his eternal kingdom. This declaration, and the message of the whole book,

[1] See Psa. 126:1, and my discussion of it in *Psalms* (Fearn: Christian Focus, 2011), vol. 2, pp. 909-10.

comes from the 'the Lord your God.' It is fitting that the book ends with reference to the covenantal LORD (*yhwh*) who assures Israel that he remains 'your God.' The final word is a re-affirmation of the covenantal relationship and this is a fitting end to messages to an erring people. God remains their God and he will carry out his purposes for them.

Application

Hints of future blessing have been given earlier in Amos' prophecy, but now the prospect is given certainty with the LORD's declaration. The hope for Israel lies in the distant future when God will raise up 'a horn of salvation for us in the house of his servant David' (Luke 1:69). Though Jesus 'was descended from David according to the flesh' he was also 'declared to be the Son of God in power according to the Spirit of holiness by his resurrection from the dead' (Rom. 1:3, 4). Failed earthly kingdoms can never be restored. What was needed is what Amos prophesied—a new kingdom that will far exceed any human expectations, and of which God is the initiator. He is the one who alone provides richly for us, bringing us safely home, and keeping us secure for eternity.

BANNER *of* TRUTH

THE Banner of Truth Trust originated in 1957 in London. The founders believed that much of the best literature of historic Christianity had been allowed to fall into oblivion and that, under God, its recovery could well lead not only to a strengthening of the church, but to true revival.

Inter-denominational in vision, this publishing work is now international, and our lists include a number of contemporary authors along with classics from the past. The translation of these books into many languages is encouraged.

A monthly magazine, *The Banner of Truth*, is also published. More information about this and all our publications can be found on our website or supplied by either of the offices below.

Head Office:
3 Murrayfield Road
Edinburgh
EH12 6EL, United Kingdom
Email: info@banneroftruth.co.uk

North America Office:
PO Box 621
Carlisle, PA 17013
United States of America
Email: info@banneroftruth.org